WAR:
4 Christian Views

Edited by Robert G. Clouse

with contributions by
Herman A. Hoyt
Myron S. Augsburger
Arthur F. Holmes
Harold O. J. Brown

InterVarsity Press
Downers Grove
Illinois 60515

InterVarsity Press is the book-publishing division of Inter-Varsity Christian Fellowship, a student movement active on campus at hundreds of universities, colleges and schools of nursing. For information about local and regional activities, write IVCF, 233 Langdon St., Madison, WI 53703.

Distributed in Canada through InterVarsity Press, 1875 Leslie St., Unit 10, Don Mills, Ontario M3B 2M5, Canada.

All Scripture quotations marked RSV are from the Revised Standard Version of the Bible, copyrighted 1946, 1952 © 1971, 1973. Other quotations are from the King James Version (KJV), The American Standard Version—1901 (ASV) and the New International Version (NIV).

ISBN 0-87784-801-7

Printed in the United States of America

Library of Congress Cataloging in Publication Data
Main entry under title:

War—four Christian views.

    Bibliography: p.
    1. Christianity and war—Addresses, essays, lectures. I. Clouse, Robert G., 1931-
II. Hoyt, Herman Arthur, 1909-
BT736.2.W344   261.8'73   81-1020
ISBN 0-87784-801-7   AACR2

18	17	16	15	14	13	12	11	10	9	8	7	6	5	4	3	2
95	94	93	92	91	90	89	88	87	86	85	84	83	82	81		

To my sons, Gary and Kenneth,
may they see the fullness of the
kingdom of God when war shall
be no more.

Introduction
Robert G. Clouse

Social problems are multiplying at a rapid pace during these closing years of the twentieth century. In addition to new issues such as environmentalism and women's rights, the age-old concerns of war, poverty and racism still plague humanity. Christians who wish to express their love to God and to their neighbors must work toward solutions to these difficulties. Of all the dilemmas that face modern society, war perhaps draws the most urgent attention because modern weaponry has made it possible for the human race to destroy itself. Also, young people who are faced with conscription must make an ethical decision with regard to personal involvement in combat.

A Biblical Debate
The Christian response to war begins with a consideration of what the Scriptures teach on the subject. The Old Testament contains many statements which have been used to support participation in armed conflict. The words of Moses in such passages as Deuteronomy 7:16 constitute a warrant

for Israel to engage in aggressive or "holy" wars to seize the Promised Land. In Deuteronomy 20:10-18 rules of conquest are given which command the Israelites to exterminate all those who live within the Holy Land. Deuteronomy, chapters seven and twenty, along with the war narratives of Joshua, Judges and Samuel, make it clear that aggressive wars were carried out "at the command of God, in the name of God and with the help of God. And even if it is argued that the Biblical 'historical' narratives have a legendary character to them, and that the wars of conquest described therein dia not actually take place, still the problem remains. For although the historical reality of the wars of conquest may perhaps be removed in this manner, the theological ideal remains."[1]

The Old Testament teaching of aggressive war has encouraged many Christians to engage in armed conflict. These individuals, however, fail to realize that Israel was a theocratic state that went to war at the command of God. In modern times there is no state whose king is God. The Israelites not only fought to take the land according to divine promise, but they also struggled to execute judgment on the wicked people who lived there. The reasons for this are cloaked in mystery because it cannot be established historically that the Canaanites were more morally corrupt than other ancient peoples. It is simply stated in the Bible that they were especially deserving of punishment. God used the Israelites to conquer them as he was later to use foreign nations to bring judgment on his own people.

Such passages as the war texts of the Old Testament remind the reader that some laws given to ancient Israel cannot be used today. The war regulations were specifically applicable to the Hebrew kingdom of God. In the teachings of Jesus the kingdom takes on a different emphasis. It is no longer confined within the boundaries of a single state but exists wherever Christ is accepted and acknowledged as Lord. The change in the form of the kingdom means that care must be taken in applying Old Testament laws to the new situation. Another point that should be noticed is that much of the Old Testament teaching emphasizes peace as well as war. In Isaiah 2:4 and similar texts the prophets presented a noble vision of a golden age when peace would come on earth not as a result of economic and cultural advances but as a gift of God.

The New Testament broadened the believer's understanding of the kingdom of God, but it has very little to say specifically on the subject of war. From its pages one must draw general principles rather than specific rules. In the Sermon on the Mount Jesus seems to teach nonresistance. The statements, "But if any one strikes you on the right cheek, turn to him the other also" (Mt. 5:39) and "Love your enemies and pray for those who persecute you" (Mt. 5:44) plainly forbid violence on the part of the followers of Christ. Yet Jesus accepted war as part of the present world system (Mt. 24:6), and his follower who was at the same time a soldier was neither condemned nor commended (Acts 10). The first disciples included Zealots, although they were encouraged to use their energies in nonpolitical efforts. Military men were also recognized in the gallery of heroes of the faith mentioned in the letter to the Hebrews (11:32). However, Jesus made it quite clear that the cause of God is not to be advanced by physical force (Jn. 18:36), and he scolded Peter for resisting the guards at his arrest (Mt. 26:52-54). The New Testament does use a number of military terms and metaphors to describe the Christian's spiritual conflict. One who accepts the lordship of Christ is a soldier (2 Tim. 2:3), who must struggle against evil (1 Pet. 2:11; Eph. 6:10-20). Although victory has been won at the cross it will not be fully realized until the return of Jesus Christ (2 Thess. 2:8).

Life in the Early Church
The quality of love found in the life and ministry of Christ was not lost in the early church. These believers saw an in-

compatibility between love and killing. Consequently, the early Christians would not serve in the Roman army. There is no evidence of a single Christian soldier after New Testament times until about A.D. 170. Because the Romans did not have universal conscription and since there was no pressure on Christians to serve, there was little need even to discuss military service. Toward the close of the second century the situation began to change and there are records of Christians in the army despite the condemnation of the theologians. Many soldiers were converted to Christianity because of the increasing popularity of Christianity, and they wondered if they should continue their military service. The faith was becoming more socially acceptable, and some felt that a person could be a model Roman as well as a follower of Christ.

Thoughtful Christians were not pleased with the blurring of distinctions between the church and the world. These people condemned participation in warfare and urged Christians to wage a spiritual conflict rather than a carnal one. Origen dealt with the problem by citing the words of Christ to Peter "For all who take the sword will perish by the sword" (Mt. 26:52). He explained that one must be wary because warfare and the vindication of our rights might lead believers to "take out the sword, [and] no such occasion is allowed by this evangelical teaching."[2] The Canons of Hippolytus, written by a Roman Christian as a guide for church discipline in the third century, indicate that a follower of Christ who is a soldier "must be taught not to kill men and to refuse to do so if he is commanded."[3] The apparent contradiction in being a soldier and not killing is resolved when one understands that it was possible for a person to be in the Roman legions for a lifetime and never kill anyone. The army performed many of the public services provided by the police force and the fire department in the twentieth century.

Believers would not join the army in the second and third centuries because it involved taking an idolatrous oath of allegiance to the emperor. The same scruples that kept Christians out of the army led them to decline to serve in other governmental positions. They refused to take part in the civil state because of the participation in sacrifices, oath taking and torture that Rome demanded of civil servants. Just as there is no evidence for the presence of Christians in the Roman army before the end of the second century, so there is no record of believers in positions of authority under the Roman government until about A.D. 250. The early followers of Christ also thought of themselves as a new community which cut across political boundaries and included all who followed the true God. In a sense they had a rival organization which replaced the old imperial ties. Because Christians regarded themselves as a separate group and did not mingle with others they were often persecuted. Their isolation led others to hate and mistrust them. When public calamities occurred they were often made the scapegoats for popular discontent.

Origen defended Christians against the charges of disloyalty which often led to persecution. His apology is found in the book *Contra Celsum,* which is a response to an elaborate attack on Christianity written about 178 by Celsus, a pagan philosopher. Celsus argued that if everyone behaved as a Christian and refused to enter the imperial forces, Rome would fall into the hands of savage barbarians and the church would be destroyed along with the rest of the classical world. Origen responded by stating that if all the Romans were converted and the barbarians invaded the Empire, it would be saved in a supernatural way. Christ promised that two or three agreeing in prayer would receive what they prayed for. Imagine what the entire Empire united in prayer could accomplish! Just as the Israelites were saved at the Red Sea while the armies of the Pharaoh were destroyed, so the Romans would be saved by divine power.

Origen, however, did not evade the dilemma of the actual situation in which the Christian minority profited from the

Roman state while seemingly not contributing to its defense. In response to this challenge he claimed that Christians gave the Empire alternative service by improving the moral fiber of society and by praying for the government. Prayer involved believers in spiritual combat against the forces of evil that caused wars and incited people to violence.

Despite the arguments of the church fathers such as Origen, the complaints of the pagans against Christianity had a basis in fact. The church benefited from Rome but tended to ignore imperial claims. This contradictory attitude could be tolerated as long as Christians were a minority within the state, but when they became more numerous and were integrated into society there was increasing pressure on them to serve in the government and the army. When Emperor Constantine made Christianity the official religion during the early fourth century, the church modified its teaching with regard to warfare. About half a century later, Augustine wrote as a product of the merger between church and state. At the time he wrote, Christians had been serving in the army for almost two hundred years, and their participation had been accepted as normal. Also, the Empire was threatened with annihilation by destructive groups of barbarians such as the Vandals. Influenced by these developments, Augustine was asked by the Roman general who commanded the armies in North Africa whether he should lead his troops in battle or retire to a monastery.

In answer, Augustine, the greatest of the Latin church fathers, laid down the teaching that a person could serve in the army and also follow the Lord. His "just war" theory consisted of rules of warfare developed by classical thinkers such as Plato and Cicero with a Christian emphasis. War, he claimed, should be fought to restore peace and to obtain justice. It must always be under the direction of the legitimate ruler and be motivated by Christian love. Such love, he believed, is not incompatible with killing because nonresistance is identified with an inward feeling. Augustine explained this position as follows:

If it is supposed that God could not enjoin warfare because in after times it was said by the Lord Jesus Christ, I say unto you, Resist not evil . . . , the answer is that what is here required is not a bodily action but an inward disposition. . . . Moses in putting to death sinners was moved not by cruelty but by love. So also was Paul when he committed the offender to Satan for the destruction of flesh. Love does not preclude a benevolent severity, nor that correction which compassion itself dictates. No one indeed is fit to inflict punishment save the one who has first overcome hate in his heart. The love of enemies admits of no dispensation, but love does not exclude wars of mercy waged by the good.[4]

Augustine also taught that a just war was to be conducted in an honorable manner. Faith was to be kept with the enemy, and there was to be no unnecessary violence, massacres, burning and looting. He emphasized that only those who held a public office or position in the army which demanded such activity were to engage in violence. Those in Christian service such as priests and monks were not allowed to take part in warfare.

Despite his rationale for the just war, Augustine felt the tension between the pacifism of the early church and the need for Christians to serve in the army. There is a gloomy mood about much of his teaching on the state. This is seen in his discussion of the Christian judge who must employ torture in the examination of accused criminals. The suspect in the case Augustine cites turns out to be innocent and has been unjustly tortured. Yet Augustine defends the participation of Christians in the practice by stating: "If then such darkness shrouds social life will the wise judge take his seat on the bench? That he will. For human society, which he cannot rightly abandon, constrains him to do his duty. He will take his seat and cry 'From my necessities deliver thou me.' "[5]

The Crusade Spirit

Despite the just war theories advanced by Augustine which seemed to harmonize participation in conflict with Christian values, the pacifism of the early church remained a living force within the community of faith. Those who killed in war were forced to do long terms of penance, and there was no glorification of the holy Christian knight until the eleventh century. The situation in Europe changed due to the break-up of the Empire and the influx of Germanic peoples. A new militant attitude was formed in the church. The Germans, as is common among most primitive groups, placed a great emphasis on warfare. Their greatest virtues, such as devotion to gods of battle and the desire to die in conflict, were those of the warrior. A fusion of the Germanic religion of war and the religion of peace took place among the Christians of Western Europe.

The most famous examples of the new warlike outlook were the Crusades. In 1095 at the Council of Clermont, in response to appeals for help from the Eastern emperor at Constantinople, Urban II preached a sermon urging his listeners to undertake an expedition under papal leadership to free the Middle East from pagan control. He stirred his audience by describing how the Turks had disemboweled Christian men, raped women and desecrated churches. Urban appealed for unity in the face of the enemy and promised forgiveness of sins for anyone who would fight to free the Holy Land. The crowd responded enthusiastically to his sermon shouting: "God wills it! God wills it!"

Historians have pointed out several reasons for the Crusades. One of these was the desire of the papacy to reduce the scale of violence in Western Europe. If the knights could not be persuaded to stop struggling with each other, perhaps they could be encouraged to fight against some other enemy.

There were really two groups involved in what was later called the First Crusade. The first of these expeditions was made up of lower-class people under the leadership of popular preachers such as Peter the Hermit. They wandered through Europe killing Jews, begging and stealing. These poverty-stricken Crusaders believed that if they could reach the land of Zion they would experience millennial conditions of peace, prosperity and joy. Many deserted the cause or died on the way, but a surprisingly large number reached Asia where the Turks massacred them. Of the thousands who started out on this "peoples" Crusade, only a few individuals survived and returned to Europe.

The second group of Crusaders was composed of nobles who understood the situation better than the poor people. Led by some of the most important men in Europe, they spent a year making preparations for their journey and arrived in Constantinople in 1097. These knights fared better than the peasants and won a series of victories which culminated in the capture of Jerusalem in 1099. An anonymous observer described the conquest of the city with these words:

> Entering the city our pilgrims pursued and killed Saracens up to the temple of Solomon, in which they had assembled and where they gave battle to us furiously for the whole day so that their blood flowed throughout the whole temple. Finally, having overcome the pagans, our knights seized a great number of men and women, and they killed whom they wished and whom they wished they let live. . . . Soon the crusaders ran throughout the city, seizing gold, silver, horses, mules, and houses full of all kinds of goods. Then rejoicing and weeping from extreme joy our men went to worship at the sepulchre of our Savior Jesus and thus fulfilled their pledge to Him.[6]

The First Crusade led to the establishment of four European states on the shores of the eastern Mediterranean. Tradition has numbered the later Crusades, but actually there was a continual coming and going of European knights to the Holy Land. The purpose of the later Crusades also changed, as one of them conquered Constantinople in 1204 and others were directed against papal foes in Europe. Even the loss of Western holdings in the eastern Mediterranean with the fall of Acre in 1291 did not stop he movement which continued into the fifteenth century.

It is clear from the Crusades that what finally overpowered the early Christian teaching against violence was not merely a just war theory but rather a merger of violence and holiness at all levels of Christian life. Many other examples could be given of the new favorable attitude taken toward violence in the church. The liturgy was expanded to include the blessing of weapons and standards. Knights were consecrated by ceremonies which often were a continuation of old pagan customs. There were even new religious orders established such as the Templars who promised to fight the enemies of God in addition to taking the normal vows of poverty, chastity and obedience. When violence became sacred, the enemy was believed to be diabolical. Thus the Muslims were looked on as the opponents of the kingdom of God, a fulfillment of the forces of the antichrist as predicted in the book of Revelation. It was considered wrong to show mercy to these enemies of God. "The code of the just war . . . was largely in abeyance in fighting the infidel. Crucifixion, ripping open those who had swallowed coins, mutilation—Bohemond of Antioch sent to the Greek Emperor a whole cargo of noses and thumbs sliced from the Saracens—such exploits the chronicles of the crusades recount without qualm. A favorite text was a verse in Jeremiah 'Cursed be he that keepeth back his hand from blood.' "[7]

Throughout the Middle Ages there was a tendency on the part of Christian writers to accept war as part of the necessary condition of society. There was little serious dispute about the necessity of fighting the Turks or the enemies of the faith in Western Europe. The just war teaching of Augustine was put into a legal form by Gratian in the twelfth century and repeated in a scholastic fashion by Thomas Aquinas during the thirteenth century. The surprising point is how little time was spent in discussing the problem. Aquinas has only one question on war in his massive theological work compared with twenty-four questions about angels.[8] At the same time the theologians were ignoring the problem of war, the growth of the chivalric ideal was exerting a powerful influence on the emerging hero image of Europeans. In *The Canterbury Tales*, Chaucer described the knight as the natural leader of the pilgrims and made him the embodiment of all that was graceful and noble in an individual.

Nationalism and Gunpowder

During the fifteenth and sixteenth centuries, several factors created a new situation in which war again received the attention of thinking Christians. Among these developments was the growth of a new technology which led to the decline of medieval methods of warfare. The most important aspect of this change was the use of gunpowder in weapons that could destroy the walls of castles and cities, thus taking away the security of the feudal lords. Later, these cannon were adopted for field use and the knight in armor was made obsolete. These changes in weaponry were grimly prophetic of further advances that would lead to the three-dimensional, nuclear warfare of the twentieth century.

Another change that affected Christian attitudes toward war during the Renaissance period was the division of Europe into dynastic monarchies from which the pattern of contemporary national states has emerged. During the sixteenth century the leading dynastic rulers were Henry VIII of England, Francis I of France and Charles V of Spain and Germany. The rivalry between these rulers destroyed the pattern in which Christians were lined up against heathen. Francis allied with the Turks against Charles, and when the pope asked the English to join in a crusade they replied that the only Turks they knew were those who lived on the other side of the English Channel.

The new style of warfare met with vigorous opposition from such leading Christian humanists as Thomas More,

Erasmus and John Colet. These individuals rediscovered the relevance of the New Testament to many matters, and this led them to condemn war. The greatest of them, Erasmus of Rotterdam (1466-1536), used his impressive talents to condemn violence. He believed renewal and reform could come to the church if individuals would study the Bible and live a simple life in imitation of Christ. To him nothing was more basic to the philosophy of Christ than hostility to war. His satire *In Praise of Folly* ridiculed the theologians who drew a justification for violence from Jesus' advice to his disciples to sell their clothes and buy swords. Whatever Jesus meant by these words he did not mean that the apostles were to fight in wars. Otherwise why did "he who so willed the sword to be brought reprehend it a little after and command it to be sheathed; and that it was never heard that the Apostles used swords and bucklers against the Gentiles, though it is likely they would have done so if Christ had ever intended as the doctors interpret."[9]

The church, Erasmus believed, had accepted the idea of the just war along with the whole body of Roman civil law which was not in harmony with the law of Christ. Also, he added, once wars are accepted as just, they tend to become glorious. In short, what he and the other humanists accused the church of doing was accepting the just war teaching, missing the true meaning of Scripture and becoming the servant of the bloodthirsty ambitions of the princes.

The era of the Renaissance was also the age of the Reformation. Despite their brilliant rediscovery of the gospel, the early Protestants did not bring peace to earth. The confessional rivalry when added to the new weapons technology resulted in bloody warfare which was not to be equaled until the twentieth century. The Protestant leaders—Luther, Zwingli and Calvin—accepted the use of violence and warfare. The European religious wars which lasted from about 1550 to 1648 seriously discredited the Reformation in many quarters. There was one group of Reformers, however, the

Anabaptists, who did not accept the use of violence. They differed widely among themselves, but were more radical than the other Protestants and rejected the state church. Beginning about 1560 they espoused pacifism because they felt Christ had initiated a new order of love and meekness in which there should be no constraint. The Christian must imitate Christ and not resist when mistreated. After all, Jesus referred to his followers as sheep: "A sheep is a suffering, defenseless, patient beast, which has no other defense save to run so long as it can and may. A sheep is no more comparable to the governance of the sword than to a wolf or lion."[10] The behavior of Christians is to be wholly different from worldly people. Said one Anabaptist leader, "Our fortress is Christ, our defense is patience, our sword is the Word of God, and our victory is the sincere, firm, unfeigned faith in Jesus Christ. Spears and swords of iron we leave to those who, alas, consider human blood and swine's blood wellnigh of equal value."[11]

In the years that followed the Peace of Westphalia (1648), which settled the last of the religious wars, dynastic states such as France under Louis XIV became the centers of power in Europe. These states suppressed local war bands and organized national standing armies. The new forces permanently replaced the nobles as the fighting element in society. At the same time the rising middle class was challenging the privileges of the old chivalric class in other fields. Faced with changing conditions, many nobles who were accustomed to warfare and had a tradition of authority took command of the growing military power of the nations. Throughout Europe in the early modern period the nobility came to monopolize the positions of command in the armed forces, and they developed a strong vested interest in increasing the military establishment. The most famous of these groups was the Junker class in Prussia. They commanded the army and formed a bureaucracy independent of the remainder of the government. The Junker-type officers of the national armies guaranteed the survival of militarism in Europe. They continued the medieval notions of chivalry military virtues and "honor."

Despite the popularity of military values, during the eighteenth century the impact of the Enlightenment and the inefficiency of the monarchies of Europe tended to check the growth of warfare. The coming of the French Revolution and the struggles that followed broke the comparative calm of the age of reason and led to the birth of modern war. The Revolution was diverted from its original goals by Napoleon (1769-1821) and transformed into an effort to conquer Europe. An artillery officer who graduated from a military academy in Paris, he skillfully manipulated the masses to form an alliance joining their democratic idealism and nationalism with the ambition and militarism of the aristocracy. He put the entire nation of France into the service of war.

Modern Warfare

The Napoleonic Wars of conquest humiliated and inspired the Prussians to copy the French methods. It was a teacher at the Prussian military academies, Karl von Clausewitz (1780-1831), whose theories of warfare were accepted as the standard in modern times. He articulated the concept of "total war," the necessity to push conflict to the "utmost bounds" of violence in order to win. As Clausewitz explained:

> He who uses force unsparingly, without reference to the bloodshed involved, must obtain a superiority if his adversary uses less vigor in its application. The former then dictates the law to the latter, and both proceed to extremities, to which the only limitations are those imposed by the amount of counteracting force on each side. . . . To introduce into a philosophy of war a principle of moderation would be an absurdity. War is an act of violence pushed to its utmost bounds.[12]

These teachings became influential throughout Europe. For example, Marshall Foch, the leader of the French army, used

Clausewitz's writings as texts in the officers college in the years before World War 1. It seems that the Prussian writer conspired with history because the Industrial Revolution of the nineteenth century greatly increased the power of armaments and made it possible to totally defeat an enemy.

Despite these ominous developments, the history of war marked time after the settlement of the Napoleonic Wars throughout most of the nineteenth century. In fact, before World War 1 broke out, there were many indications that international cooperation and humanitarianism might reduce the need for conflict. There was a strong Christian influence that led to international gatherings such as the Hague Conferences of 1899 and 1907. From these meetings came decisions that limited the nature of war, protected the rights of prisoners of war, affirmed the need to care for the sick and the wounded, promised protection of private property and guaranteed the rights of neutrals.

These principles were violated by both sides during World War 1. Despite the fact that the war was not fought over basic ideological issues, it became necessary to use these ideas to justify the slaughter and monotony of the seemingly endless "war effort." Clausewitz's total or absolute war could now be fought due to technological advances. Modern artillery, extensive use of mines, machine guns, poison gas, submarine warfare and aerial bombardment broke the rules of war so confidently set forth at the Hague Conference of 1907. Economic warfare and blockades which led to widespread food shortages affected millions of people who were not soldiers in the traditional sense. War became three-dimensional, and its capability to strike at civilian populations was vastly increased. The conflict had started with a great deal of lighthearted, irresponsible patriotic fervor, and Christians joined in the spirit. Later the mood toughened and many came to agree with the English churchman who exhorted the troops to

Kill Germans—to kill them, not for the sake of killing, but

to save the world, to kill the good as well as the bad, to kill the young men as well as the old, to kill those who have shown kindness to our wounded as well as those fiends who crucified the Canadian Sergeant.... As I have said a thousand times, I look upon it as a war for purity, I look upon everyone who dies in it as a martyr.[13]

The governments managed to drag their people through the war, but the armistice only laid the basis for another conflict. While totalitarian regimes grew in Germany, Japan and Russia, the mood turned to discouragement in much of the Western world. An attitude of pacifist resignation grew in the liberal democracies of Europe, and the United States became isolationist. Under the League of Nations, which was formed to stop a repetition of World War 1, collective security and peaceful settlement of disputes were to control international relations. But a world government without the full support of its members could not operate successfully. So a Second World War came and brought even more severe horrors. That war differed from World War 1 because it was a battle to the end between different, antagonistic social and political systems. The demand for unconditional surrender and the rejection of a negotiated peace demonstrates the triumph of the logic of violence. To achieve the total suppression of the enemy, the techniques of violence were perfected. New rockets and nuclear weapons were produced that seemed to represent the ultimate in destructive capabilities. With the end of World War 2, the threat to world peace continued in the rivalry between the United States and the U.S.S.R. The arms race became a part of everyday life, and the satisfaction of "defense" needs has been woven into the very texture of industrial technological society. As one writer warns:

What is unique about the present situation is that, partly through culpable negligence and partly through sheer lack of understanding, we have allowed the primitive pattern of total enmity to grow to its full natural dimensions and to become incorporated in the very fabric of a complex civilization developing in a way increasingly beyond our control. The result of this is that we are now faced with massive structural problems which cannot be solved simply in terms of their origins.[14]

Four Basic Views

This brief survey reveals several reactions on the part of Christians toward war. These can be categorized as Christian pacifism or nonresistance, the just war and the crusade. The early church, which has been an ideal for believers, took a pacifist view toward violence. Other groups such as the humanists and the Anabaptists have also followed this teaching. Most Christian groups, however, have agreed with Augustine and preached that certain wars are justified. While some churches such as the Church of the Brethren, the Quakers and the Mennonites, maintain a pacifist stance, most of the major denominations including the Lutherans, Presbyterians, Baptists, Roman Catholics, Methodists and Reformed adhere to the just war interpretation. And some individuals have become convinced of the absolute evil of the enemy and advocated a crusade. The leaders of medieval society in the eleventh to the fifteenth century came to feel that way toward the Turks. During the First World War many Christians in the United States and Western Europe looked on Germany in the same way. Billy Sunday claimed that if you turned the pot of hell upside down you would find "made in Germany" stamped on the bottom.[15] Today many Christians feel that Communism is so evil that the West must engage in war with Russia.

Because many readers of this book may be called upon to serve in the military if there is another large-scale conflict, it is important to try to arrive at some conclusion about war. Each of the interpretations presented here have devout evangelical Christian adherents. The following essays are offered as statements of these positions by believers who hold the view toward war and peace that they express. Herman A. Hoyt, president emeritus of Grace Theological Seminary, writes about nonresistance from the standpoint of one who feels that a person may engage in noncombatant service in the armed forces. Professor Myron S. Augsburger, former president of Eastern Mennonite College, presents the case for a thoroughgoing Christian pacifism which would lead the believer to refuse military induction or support. Arthur F. Holmes is professor of Philosophy at Wheaton College and a supporter of the just war who feels that Christians must be willing to cooperate in national life and fight in the armed forces if necessary. In the last essay Harold O. J. Brown, professor of systematic theology at Trinity Evangelical Divinity School, discusses the crusade or preventive war in which Christians are to fight eagerly. At the conclusion of each of the articles the other contributors respond from their individual viewpoints. After my concluding remarks, there is a selected bibliography on war, peace and the Christian.

It is my hope that these essays and discussions will help readers to formulate their own views about war. We have already stated that armed conflict may be the most pressing problem that global society faces today. Those who follow Jesus Christ must seek to understand his will in relationship to matters of war and peace.

Nonresistance

Nonresistance

Herman A. Hoyt

The exercise of physical force has characterized the course of history since the entrance of sin into the human family. Expulsion from the Garden of Eden was followed almost immediately by the sin of Cain when he slew his brother (Gen. 4:8). He then became the object of physical wrath in the society of that day (Gen. 4:14-15). His descendants followed the path he made, so physical violence became a way of life (Gen. 4:23-24). This pattern of life grew to such enormous proportions that God was forced to bring the flood on humanity (Gen. 6:13).

From that day till this hour the pages of history are replete with the accounts of violence in ever-expanding proportions. Personal animosities, family feuds, racial strife, class conflict, religious hatreds, civil hostilities and national conflagration have all resulted in the use of physical force. The mounting dimensions of armed might and military operations have now reached the point where they threaten the

existence of civilization and, perhaps even more, the survival of humanity. Even so, the development of war on a global
scale continues, and as the instruments of conflict increase
in size and destructiveness it means that the worst is yet
ahead.

It is this frightening prospect that has produced a veritable
contagion of efforts by nations to halt the toboggan slide toward world destruction. The past one hundred years, more
particularly the last seventy-five years and even more precisely the last thirty years, have been marked by every conceivable tactic known to halt the trend toward total annihilation. There have been alliances to maintain a balance of
power, world courts, disarmament conferences, the League
of Nations, the United Nations, détente, NATO, SEATO,
SALT talks. All to no avail. The Middle East crisis threatens
to engulf the whole world. In the face of demands made by
the Arabs, Israel has two alternatives. On the one hand Israel
can resist the pressures of the Arabs, realizing this course
will lead inevitably to war. On the other hand, she can yield
to these pressures and face annihilation.

These prospects mean that an ever-increasing involvement
of the church in the wars of nations lies ahead. From its beginning at Pentecost, the church has been forced to face the
realities of armed strife. During the first three hundred years,
this was minimal. But when Christianity became the religion
of the Roman Empire, the possibilities of personal involvement increased. Yet still, as long as armies were made up of
mercenaries, there was a possibility of avoiding armed
service. At the time of the Reformation, however, Luther and
Calvin identified church and state, and Christian involvement in military service increased.

It was during Napoleon's time that the situation became
serious for Christians. He inaugurated nationwide conscription. While this did not spread to the New World until much
later, there was a feeling among the American colonists that
Christians should not be exempt from military service. They

were, however, permitted to pay money in lieu of military service. In addition they were expected to pay a special war tax and to contribute to the needs of the army and the alleviation of suffering.

By the time of the Civil War, universal military conscription had become the pattern of government across the world. It was slow in being employed during the War Between the States, and even after it was made law in both North and South, Christians were permitted to pay for a substitute. World War 1 saw a definite change. Universal conscription was made absolute. No substitutes were allowed nor could a person pay a fee. Every man had to answer the draft in person. When the law covering conscription was finally passed, it did make provision for conscientious objection, but defined noncombatancy as being under military direction.

In World War 2 the government provided greater opportunity for exemption from military service. Not only were religious scruples made a basis for relief from military service, but philosophic considerations were also given a place for evaluation. The Korean War and the war in Viet Nam brought new pressures on the government to re-evaluate the stipulations involved in universal military conscription. Without a doubt any war of the future will develop demands upon the men and women of this country commensurate with the emergency. This is then the time to give new thought to the proper Christian position to take in the next emergency. Calm reflection will be more apt to produce right thinking and response than opinions formed in the wildfire of emotion.

The Doctrine of Nonresistance

I have come to the conclusion that the Bible teaches nonresistance on the part of Christians. It is unfortunate that the term *nonresistance* has been given to this doctrine. This gives the impression of something altogether negative and passive. The name comes from the words of Matthew 5:39,

"That ye *resist not* evil" (italics mine; KJV used primarily throughout this essay). Contrary to what the name suggests, the practice is very positive and active. Seven elements are involved in the concept of *nonresistance*.

1. Nonresistance is one aspect of the biblical teaching on separation from the world. One of the first things a saved person is commanded to do is to separate himself from the practices of this world. Paul admonishes him to "be not conformed to this world" (Rom. 12:2). This covers all practices of life that make up the pattern of this present evil age and that would conceal the new nature within. Inasmuch as true Christians are "not of this world" (Jn. 17:16), but have been chosen by Christ out of the world (Jn. 15:19), it is the divine purpose to keep them from the evil in the world (Jn. 17:15). One of those evils is the exercise of physical force to accomplish the purposes of life. This includes the use of force in times of peace and also in times of war.

2. It becomes clear from the basic injunction on separation that there is a definite separation of church and state according to the divine Word. Christ declared to Pilate, "My kingdom is not of this world" (Jn. 18:36). Paul explained that all those who name the name of Christ and experience the miracle of regeneration have been translated into the kingdom of Jesus Christ (Col. 1:13; Jn. 3:3, 5). They are no longer of this world even as Christ is not of this world (Jn. 17:16). They now have citizenship in heaven (Phil. 3:20 ASV), and it is their responsibility to live like pilgrims and strangers in the world (Heb. 11:8-16). Their conduct should be conditioned by the pattern of the kingdom of the heavens.

3. Since the church and state belong to separate kingdoms or spheres of operation, the methods for defense and offense should also be different. Christ was patently clear on this point in addressing Pilate. "If my kingdom were of this world, then would my servants fight, that I should not be delivered to the Jews: but now is my kingdom not from hence" (Jn. 18:36). This means that believers are not free to

employ physical force as a method of warfare. They cannot "war after the flesh: For the weapons of our warfare are not carnal" (2 Cor. 10:3-4). But this is not to depreciate the weapons available to the Christian, for they are "mighty through God to the pulling down of strong holds" (2 Cor. 10:4).

4. On the basis of the foregoing points, it follows that physical violence is forbidden to believers as a method of accomplishing a purpose. A careful examination of Matthew 5:38-48 leads to the conclusion that physical violence is not Christian. In the light of the fact that the believer is urged to follow the example of Christ this conclusion is made even more emphatic (1 Jn. 2:6). We are exhorted "to walk, even as he walked," and to "follow his steps: Who did no sin, neither was guile found in his mouth: Who, when he was reviled, reviled not again; when he suffered, he threatened not; but committed himself to him that judgeth righteously: Who his own self bare our sins in his own body on the tree" (1 Pet. 2:21-24).

5. Where physical violence is forbidden for any purpose, it is made only too clear that believers have no right to use physical violence in the propagation of the Christian faith. This does not mean that believers are without power for accomplishing the task that has been committed to them. For the gospel itself is the power of God unto salvation (Rom. 1:16). As an added encouragement believers are instructed that "Ye shall receive power, after that the Holy Ghost is come upon you" (Acts 1:8). And this power provides the weapons of our warfare that are "mighty through God to the pulling down of strong holds" (2 Cor. 10:4). Whenever the church has turned aside from this equipment and used physical force to enlarge her borders nothing but reproach and ruin has resulted.

6. What has been true in using force to extend the church has also been true when the church joined the nations of the world in the exercise of force. This situation has produced an incongruity that has aroused criticism even from

unbelievers. If believers belong to the kingdom of Christ, then they do not belong to the kingdom of the world. And if it is wrong for believers to employ physical force to advance spiritual interests, then it is also wrong for believers to join the world in the use of physical force to achieve temporal interests. The words of Christ come with tremendous power at this point: "If my kingdom were of this world, then would my servants fight . . . but now is my kingdom not from hence" (Jn. 18:36).

7. Lest we draw an incorrect conclusion, let me say that even though believers are forbidden the use of physical force to accomplish a temporal end, they are still obligated to exercise spiritual means to do good and to bring blessing to others. Jesus left no doubt in the minds of his disciples both by example (1 Pet. 2:21-24), exhortation (Mt. 5:38-48) and apostolic instruction, that believers are responsible to display good and stand against evil by spiritual means (Rom. 12:17-21; 13:8). While it is not easy to resist evil by spiritual means, Christians are left with no other alternative (Jas. 4:7; 1 Pet. 5:9; Eph. 6:10-13).

Underlying Principles
Up to this point the explicit teaching of Scripture on the doctrine of nonresistance has been set forth. But certain underlying principles run through all the passages dealing with this subject. It is necessary to call these to our attention.

1. *The doctrine of nonresistance is biblical* and is clearly taught in the Word of God. This was the practice of the early church up until A.D. 174.[1] From that point on the changing circumstances of the church and human traditions began to invade the thinking of believers.[2] Except for isolated instances the church gradually drew away from the original position as set forth in the New Testament. This situation continued through the Reformation and up until the pietistic movement in central Europe and England. With the Bible in the hands of more people, the doctrine of nonresistance

was recovered and has been practiced by segments of the Christian church up to the present.[3]

2. *There are four passages in the New Testament that treat nonresistance specifically.* Matthew 5:38-48 provides the basis for the name given to this doctrine. This passage was given to limit the extent of retaliation in the exercise of justice. It is so much a part of the old nature to repay a wrong with more than one has suffered, that in the Old Testament and repeated in the New Testament, requital is limited. In fact, in place of revenge, the believer is to impart good. This is Christlike and Christian. A passage in Luke 6:27-36 parallels the one in Matthew except that it gives a larger emphasis on the positive side of communicating good to the enemy. Paul touches on this subject in his letter to the Romans: "Avenge not yourselves, but rather give place unto wrath .... Owe no man any thing, but to love one another" (Rom. 12:19-21; 13:8). To support his instruction on this point, Peter cites the example of Christ (1 Pet. 2:18-24).

On the basis of these Scriptures, four observations can be made.

(a) Spiritual principles for guiding the believer are set forth in these Scriptures. Strict retaliation was provided for and permitted under the Old Testament Law (Ex. 21:23-25). This is repeated in the Sermon on the Mount. But even this was not the highest and best method of justice. If the highest measure of good was to come to everyone, it must be recognized that underlying the Old Testament Law there was the second great commandment: "Thou shalt love thy neighbour as thyself" (Lev. 19:18; Mt. 22:39). Jesus emphasized this in his teaching. Under grace the whole motive of social relations is changed. The Author of the law has come and, seeing how men have misunderstood and misused the law, he now declares: "But I say unto you, Resist not him that is evil" (Mt. 5:39 ASV). That which was implicit in the Old Testament Law is now made explicit in Jesus' teaching. Vengeance belongs to the Lord (Rom. 12:19), and believers are exhorted to love their enemies (Mt. 5:38-48; Lk. 6:27-36; Rom. 12:19-21; 13:8-14; 1 Pet. 2:1-24).

(b) In every one of these Scriptures the subject and emphasis is on the personal conduct of individual believers. The very nature of each exhortation is such that only individual believers could be meant to respond to the teaching. These commands are not delivered to groups, congregations, governments or nations. Any careful examination of the language makes this a necessary conclusion. The "whosoever" and "if any man" individualizes the command. Even if these expressions did not appear, and a whole congregation were being addressed, the only way for these exhortations to be carried out would be by the personal effort of individual believers. The individualizing principle of these Scriptures makes application to governments and nations wholly illogical. Never is the message of the New Testament directed to unregenerate worldly governments.

(c) In every one of these Scriptures some aspect of the exercise of physical force is considered. Resistance against spiritual evil is not in view here, though it is certainly discussed at length in many other places in the New Testament. In every case where spiritual evil is the subject of discussion believers are called upon to resist it, and to do so in a spiritual way (Eph. 6:10-13; Jas. 4:7; 1 Pet. 5:9). Overcoming physical evil with spiritual good is the thrust of these passages.

(d) Moreover, these Scriptures set forth spiritual ideals which will be universally realized when the kingdom of God is established on earth. Today Christ is calling out a spiritual aristocracy who will someday experience the kingdom in its physical reality. But inasmuch as they are now subjects of that kingdom, they should display the spiritual characteristics that will someday be universally realized (Mt. 5:3; Lk. 6:20). Possessing a "blessed" or born-again nature constitutes the right to enter that kingdom. And if this nature is present, then it ought to exhibit the characteristics now.

The night of sin is far spent and the day is at hand, so true
believers ought to be living in nonconformity with the world
and as strangers and pilgrims on earth (Rom. 13:11-12; 1 Pet.
2:11). The coming of Christ and the establishing of his kingdom on earth is strong incentive to display spiritual characteristics now.

3. *The obligations of nonresistance are laid upon believers only.* If you go back over the various Scriptures dealing
with nonresistance, it will be perfectly clear that each passage is directed to the people of God. The "blessed" people
are those to whom Christ directs his Word as set forth in
Matthew 5:3-10 and Luke 6:20. The word *blessed* in the
original relates to character, condition and consciousness
within, not to a bestowal of blessing from without. It is
almost comparable with the expression *born again.* It is
used especially to describe the nature of God (1 Tim. 1:11;
6:15). The descriptions *brethren* and *dearly beloved* denote
the people to whom Paul wrote (Rom. 12:1, 19). Peter certainly had Christians in mind when he addressed the "dearly
beloved" and insisted that they should behave as "strangers
and pilgrims" in the earth (1 Pet. 2:11).

(a) It follows then that the Scriptures were not in any
sense directed toward unsaved men. The only way that the
Scriptures could possibly reach the unbelieving world is
through the ministry of the saved. It is in this way that the
warning of impending judgment reaches the lost, and it is the
saved who communicate the gracious entreaty of Christ to
be saved. If the lost respond to the warning of judgment and
the invitation to be saved, then the New Testament speaks to
them directly. But in such instances they now are the children of God. To them in this changed spiritual condition the
obligations of nonresistance apply. Thus, the Bible is always
and primarily a message for the people of God, instructing
them in what to believe, exhorting them to walk according
to the truth and encouraging them in the midst of trial and
suffering. If this fact is comprehended it will safeguard

believers from some of the errors which bear upon the doctrine of nonresistance.

(b) Moreover, the doctrine of nonresistance is not a plank in some political platform. Examine the passages to which continuous reference has been made and it will become clear that the writers were not setting one form of government over against another, or one nation over against another. In the same context of some of these passages the writer is enjoining believers to be subject to the government under which they live. Christ urges Jews to "render therefore unto Caesar the things which are Caesar's," but while doing that, not to forget to render "to God, the things that are God's" (Mt. 22:21). Paul speaks in the same vein. "Let every soul be subject unto the higher powers. For there is no power but of God: the powers that be are ordained of God" (Rom. 13:1). And Peter follows the same pattern in exhorting believers: "Submit yourselves to every ordinance of man for the Lord's sake: whether it be to the king, as supreme; Or unto governors, as unto them that are sent by him for the punishment of evildoers, and for the praise of them that do well.... Honour the king" (1 Pet. 2:13-14, 17). Such passages indicate that nonresistance is a spiritual principle intended for individual believers under any form of government.

(c) Again it must be recognized that nonresistance is not a part of some merely social program. No careful student of the Scriptures will deny that nonresistance has social implications. The very nature of nonresistance is intended to be felt in the social realm. But on the other hand, the doctrine of nonresistance is not primarily social. The basic significance of nonresistance is spiritual, and the social is merely the outward display or by-product. For instance, the purpose of Matthew 5:38-48 is to demonstrate that those who practice nonresistance are "blessed" (5:3-10); that is, born-again people who are the children of God (5:45). Luke emphasizes this same thing (Lk. 6:27-36). Paul's instruction on dealing with enemies (Rom. 12:19-21) is so that believers will show they do not belong to this world (Rom. 12:2). Peter's injunction harmonized with the preceding Scriptures that Christians should regard themselves as strangers and pilgrims in this present world system (1 Pet. 2:11).

(d) In addition to the above, nonresistance is not a chance inconsistency in the New Testament theological system. Some religious groups have a sound theological system until they deal with nonresistance. At this point they lose sight of what they have affirmed. The system clearly argues for the separation of church and state, but at this point they project the church and believers back into the state. They do not see that the kingdom of Christ and the kingdom of this world operate in two different spheres. They claim that nonresistance is also for the nations of the world and for human governments during this age. It appears that they do not have a clear picture of the prophetic program for the future. They expect humanity to be the great factor in the establishing of the kingdom of God on earth. But in the teaching of Christ and the letters of Paul and Peter it is clear that the kingdom of God will be established by the supernatural, catastrophic and sovereign appearing of the great God and Savior Jesus Christ. This method of setting up the kingdom will be necessary because human government will resist the grace and love of God to the last. Even people belonging to the professing but false church will join in one final religious rebellion at the end of time (2 Thess. 2:3).

This leaves the doctrine of nonresistance right where the writers of the New Testament intended it to be; namely, as a spiritual principle to be exercised by the people of God in the midst of this wicked world. Whenever an entire nation reaches the point that all within its boundaries are Christian and are practicing the principle of nonresistance it may be fairly concluded that the kingdom of God has been established on earth. This will be true only when Christ has returned and by his almighty power set up his kingdom and purged all those unfit for it (Mt. 13:37-43; 25:31-46 NASB).

4. *The doctrine of nonresistance harmonizes with the entire teaching of the New Testament.* Nonresistance is part of a perfect, systematic, logical system which commends itself to the thinking Christian.

(a) This doctrine harmonizes with the life and ministry of Christ while on earth. His name was called Jesus because he would save his people from their sins (Mt. 1:21). At his coming there was good news for all people (Lk. 2:10-11). He came to seek and save the lost (Lk. 19:10). He came to save and not to destroy (Lk. 9:54-56). He went about doing good and healing (Acts 10:38). When he was reviled he did not respond in kind, but "bare our sins in his own body on the tree" (1 Pet. 2:24). These passages demonstrate that the whole life and ministry of Christ was one of nonresistance. Believers are exhorted to follow his example (1 Pet. 2:21) and to walk as he walked (1 Jn. 2:6).

Only upon two occasions does Christ seem to follow a course inconsistent with his regular pattern of life. These relate to the cleansing of the temple (Jn. 2:13-16; Mt. 21:12-13). But it has not been proven that on these occasions he used physical force on men. He did on the beasts, but there is no indication that men were the objects of physical force. Even if they were, however, Jesus was merely exercising the sovereign authority of his messianic office and giving people a glimpse of the vengeance that will be inflicted when he returns to execute divine wrath.

(b) This doctrine harmonizes with the divine program of eschatology set forth in the Bible. Eschatology is that system of teaching which outlines the various events with which the present age will come to its close. At that time the day of man will be terminated and the day of the Lord ushered in. During the day of man, God is permitting men to go their way, but offering them his grace and love. But at Christ's coming the Lord will take full charge of events. The saved will be raptured into the presence of Christ (1 Thess. 4:13-18). Vengeance will be meted out on the wicked (Rom. 12:19;

1 Thess. 4:6; Heb. 10:30; 2 Thess. 1:5-9; Jas. 5:7-9). This recompense upon the wicked will be effected at the coming of Christ in glory (Rev. 19:11-21). Because vengeance is yet to come, believers are to be patient unto the coming of the Lord (Jas. 5:7-9). It is therefore necessary for believers to practice nonresistance as they look for the return of Christ and the execution of vengeance.

(c) It is a striking fact that this doctrine harmonizes with the great plan Christ laid out for his church during this age. Anything that would contradict or counteract that plan should be regarded as inconsistent and inimical to the program of Christ. Opposition to nonresistance prevents the realization of that program, and believers must oppose such actions. Witnessing for him to the salvation of souls is one aspect of his program (Acts 1:8; Mt. 28:19-20). This is the supreme business of the church. Inasmuch as the kingdom was to be delayed for some time, the interim was to be filled with witnessing in preparation for that event. Witnessing was for the purpose of gathering an aristocracy for that kingdom from all the nations of the world. Believers were to give themselves unreservedly to this task. Military service would exhaust their time and effort, but nonresistance would provide them with opportunity to obey. In addition to witnessing, the believer is called to Christlike conduct. Nonresistance is one of the things Christ urged believers to observe (Mt. 28:20). Any system that encourages the believer to behave in a manner opposed to what Christ taught cannot be regarded as right and proper. Moreover, believers were enjoined to point people to the coming of Christ when their ideals and hopes will be realized. He is preparing a home for the saved where all sorrow will vanish and the deepest joy will be experienced (Jn. 14:1-3). Affections should therefore be set on things above, where the sons of God will be manifested in glory (Col. 3:1-4). Someday, the eternal city with foundations whose builder and maker is God will be realized on earth (Heb. 11:10, 13-16; 13:13-14). The puny efforts of men and women expended in war will never achieve this. How logical then for believers to reserve all their efforts for the realization of this goal by following the command of Christ in nonresistance.

(d) It is amazing that the doctrine of nonresistance harmonizes with various commands Christ gave to believers which otherwise could not be carried out. These statements are far more numerous than those that have already been discussed. It will be sufficient to cite just a few. The doctrine of nonresistance harmonizes with the command of Christ for believers to love their enemies (Mt. 5:44; Lk. 6:27; Rom. 12:20; 13:8-10), to return good for evil (Rom. 12:17, 21; 1 Pet. 3:9), to do good to all people (Rom. 12:17; Gal. 6:10), to make no provision for the flesh (Rom. 13:13-14) and to follow after things which make for peace (Rom. 12:18; 14:19).

5. *The doctrine of nonresistance rests upon certain important principles.*

(a) The kingdom of Christ is not of this world, and therefore the subjects of this kingdom should not employ force to maintain it (Jn. 18:36). The nature and source of this kingdom together with those who are its subjects argue for some method other than physical violence for defending it.

(b) The Spirit of Christ is not of this world, and therefore those who possess that Spirit cannot use carnal methods. James and John requested the privilege of calling down fire on the enemies of the Lord in Samaria, as Elijah did, "But he turned, and rebuked them, and said, Ye know not what manner of spirit ye are of. For the Son of man is not come to destroy men's lives, but to save them" (Lk. 9:55-56). One of the first fruits of the Spirit is peace, and those who possess that Spirit should be peacemakers (Gal. 5:22; Mt. 5:9). It would therefore be impossible for men who possess the Spirit to take up arms in hostility.

(c) The purpose of Christ is not of this world, for he did not come to destroy men's lives, but to save them (Lk. 9:56). If Christians promote that purpose they cannot possibly take human life. Taking life is destroying that which people hold most precious, and it eliminates the opportunity for hearing the Word of Christ and being eternally saved from both physical and spiritual ruin.

(d) The methods of Christ are not of this world, for he does not use carnal weapons in his warfare. "For though we walk in the flesh, we do not war after the flesh: (For the weapons of our warfare are not carnal, but mighty through God to the pulling down of strong holds;)" (2 Cor. 10:3-4). Probably no one has ever yet endured more reviling and persecution than Christ. And yet never once did he resort to carnal weapons for defense. As a class of individuals the same thing may be said of Christians across the centuries. They have won their battles by the message of grace and by their kindly manner of life.

(e) The evaluations of Christ are not of this world, for he penetrates to the ultimate meanings of life. "For whosoever will save his life shall lose it; but whosoever shall lose his life for my sake and the gospel's, the same shall save it" (Mk. 8:35; Jn. 12:25). The sense of these passages is ultimately spiritual, but the outcome turns on the attitude one takes toward life in this world and the methods used to save that life. If existence in this world is more important than life with Christ, then one belongs to this world and will employ the world's methods to save one's life. But the outcome will be loss of life both physically and spiritually. On the other hand, if one is willing to lose his life for the sake of Christ and the gospel, he will use the methods of Christ, and the outcome will be the saving of life both physically and spiritually.

(f) The protection of Christ is not of this world, but is heavenly and eternal. Divine care operates within the sphere of and the control of the sovereign will of God. Even though Christ was in the hands of hostile Jews, he could encourage his disciples by saying, "Thinkest thou that I cannot now pray to my Father, and he shall presently give me more than twelve legions of angels? But how then shall the scriptures be fulfilled, that thus it must be?" (Mt. 26:53-54). Christ came to fulfill the will of God and at this point it meant that he must die (Mt. 20:28).

In the case of others it was the will of God to protect them by various means. He rescued Peter from prison by angelic intervention (Acts 5:19); later Peter and John were saved by public sentiment (Acts 5:26); and still later they were delivered by the reasoning of a great Jewish teacher (Acts 5:38-39). The twelfth chapter of Acts recounts how God allowed James to suffer martyrdom (12:2), but Peter was saved from death by the prayers of the saints (Acts 12:3-17).

Those who practice nonresistance are in the center of God's perfect will. The outcome rests with Christ. Some may have to pay with their lives for the privilege and determination to follow the commands of Christ. Others may be rescued from mortal danger by various means under the control of God. But in either case the obedient servant will bear a vigorous and lasting testimony to the grace of God.

Pacifism and Biblical Nonresistance
Today many different types of nonresistance are clamoring for attention, and they often appear to be similar to biblical nonresistance. The outward resemblances have led many people to place them all in the same class. But there are precise and sharp differences when they are examined more closely. The sources out of which they arise, the systems they develop, their essential significance and the service they are designed to achieve are clearly distinguished from biblical nonresistance. In general there are four types of pacifism; philosophic, political, social, religious. These are not synonymous with biblical nonresistance.

Philosophic pacifism is comparatively new. Though it may have existed before, it did not make an appreciable impression on society until the Second World War. It does not base its teaching on biblical or religious principles. For reasons that are sometimes called spiritual or moral, the advocates of this type of pacifism insist that war is wrong. There is no effort to organize movements against the government, however. This is largely a personal, individual effort when confronted with conscription into the armed services. Such people insist that compulsory military service is an infringement on the human rights and liberties provided by the Constitution of the United States. They are perfectly willing for governments to wage war, and in most cases will support the conflict, but they want the right to be exempt from personal participation. It is not difficult to see that this position is based purely on human reason, and is therefore to be distinguished from biblical nonresistance which bases its convictions on divine revelation.

Political pacifism confines itself largely to the sphere of government and international relations. In recent years this type of pacifism has provided fertile ground for the propaganda of subversive organizations. Communistic elements within the U.S. have used this as a steppingstone to hinder the upgrading of armed might and potential for protecting the country against hostile nations. The desire for peace and for an escape from the heavy burden of taxation which military preparations demand are skillfully used to promote this outlook. Such groups as The American League for Peace and Democracy and The American League Against War and Fascism for alleged political and ideological reasons promote this program. They are determined to undermine the government and make the nation vulnerable to attack by foreign powers.[4] Undiscerning patriotic citizens of the United States have classed biblical nonresistance with this type of pacifism and have been aroused to righteous indignation.

But any careful scrutiny of the differences between biblical nonresistance and political pacifism will reveal that the pattern and purposes are entirely at odds. Biblical nonresistance derives its authority from the Bible and does not seek to undermine the government, while political pacifism is based on human reason alone and is utterly subversive.

Social pacifism is perhaps the most dangerous type in existence today. It operates largely in the religious area but combines the political in its ideological system. Religious liberalism is infiltrated with this approach to war. The leaders in this movement are largely theologians who deny the eschatology of the Bible. They argue that no thinking Christian could possibly accept the prospect for the future as set forth in the prophetic Scriptures. In their estimation all that is left of biblical truth is the grace of God. After almost two thousand years they feel it has accomplished very little for society. In this late hour the world has experienced the greatest wars, the severest famines, the most widespread poverty and the most devastating diseases. They argue that in this day of enlightenment and scientific advance it is time for a new interpretation of Scripture. In the place of the eschatological hope as set forth in the Bible, the church should now develop a hope for humanity by entering into industrial relations, political affiliations, international connections and community socialization. This is the social gospel with its emphasis on human betterment, the alleviation of suffering, the reduction of poverty and the complete abolition of war. It is not difficult to see how those who hold the social gospel make an easy prey to Communism. Communism holds out a false hope that by human effort a glorious kingdom can at last be realized.

But biblical nonresistance is not to be identified with this type of pacifism. The social pacifists have apostatized. They not only deny the eschatology of the Bible, but also pervert the doctrine of the grace of God so that the entire Bible is lost to the believer. But more than that, they undermine the government of the land and lay a foundation for its eventual overthrow. Those who believe in scriptural nonresistance, however, hold tenaciously to the entire Bible and do not pervert the doctrine of grace by which salvation comes. As true adherents to the Word of God, they teach patriotism and obedience to the government.

Religious pacifism is held by Christian groups who are sincerely dedicated to the Bible. These believers do not repudiate the Scriptures, but they are inconsistent in their interpretation of the Bible's teaching about war. Their eschatology provides the basis for these inconsistencies. Starting with the position that war is wrong, they have decided that it is wrong even for nations of this world and therefore they should oppose the war effort in their own nation. They have refused to buy bonds, participate in the mobilization effort, enter into the armed services in any capacity, or even pray for the nation.

Since there are many groups who fall into this class, several variations of this sort of pacifism exist and they are not easily classified. However, in almost every case they draw their reasoning from Scripture. Two errors of interpretation can be discovered in their theological systems. The first is the failure to understand that the church is completely separated from the state. Even though they give lip service to this tenet of the faith, they proceed in their thinking as though it did not exist. They identify church and state and, since the former has no authority to employ armed might, they conclude that this is also true for the state.

The second error is the failure to comprehend the prophetic picture of the consummation of the age. The Word of God promises the establishing of a kingdom on earth at the coming of Christ. That coming may take place at any moment. Therefore the Christian should be enthusiastically expecting Christ's return and witnessing for him as the opportunity arises. Christians can therefore perform their responsibilities to the government in everything except participation in armed conflict and let war take its course knowing that shortly Christ will come and usher in the age of peace. These groups do not follow the Scripture at this point, feeling that it is their responsibility to oppose war now and by human effort to help usher in the age of peace.

Failure to see clearly the scriptural teaching on these two points has made religious pacifists easy prey for modern religious liberalism. The leaven of liberalism is gradually taking its course and is working havoc in many areas. But in other areas there is a desperate effort being made to cling to the Word of God and demonstrate this fact by a pacifism which they feel is biblical.

Biblical nonresistance must not be identified with any of the above forms of pacifism. Nonresistance recognizes that the Bible teaches the separation of church and state and that each has its place in this age. Biblical nonresistance also recognizes that believers should be separated from the things of this world, and therefore they should be separated from the use of weapons in the taking of human life. But nonresistance recognizes that God permits human governments to exercise force for the protection of lives and property. War is wrong, but armed might is the one final argument understood by sinful men and the one to which they ultimately bow. That was the reason why in the inauguration of human government following the flood God ordained that physical force could be used to establish its authority (Gen. 9:5-6).

Biblical nonresistance holds that the Christians have a responsibility to the government (Rom. 12:1-7). They should obey the state in everything that is good. They should pay taxes, pray for those in authority and submit themselves to every law that does not ask them to do anything contrary to the higher law of God (Acts 4:17-20; 5:28-29). Taking human life is clearly prohibited by the law of God (Ex. 20:13). At this point believers must respectfully refuse to comply with the regulations of military operation. But believers are free to serve their country in the army or under civilian direction in anything that is good. There are multitudes of things that need the dedicated and efficient service of men and women in the armed services. As noncombatants, believers can serve in the medical corps and as chaplains, to encourage the sick and dying and bear a personal witness to the saving grace of our blessed Lord. In this way they can serve their country and at the same time faithfully discharge their responsibilities as Christians in everything that pertains to life and goodliness.

Some Problems

The unbelieving world usually denies the validity of the doctrine of nonresistance. This should not surprise the Christian for he or she understands that the natural man receives not the things of the Spirit of God, neither can he know them for they are spiritually discerned (1 Cor. 2:14). Like Christ and the children of God, the doctrine of nonresistance is so utterly contrary to the thinking and practice of unregenerate men that they cannot understand it (1 Jn. 3:1).

But when the Christian sees that the larger part of professing Christendom also rejects this teaching as an integral part of the Word of God, then there is reason for real concern. Protestantism as a whole, and especially the evangelical Protestantism of today, is vigorously opposed to the doctrine of nonresistance. In times of war evangelicals join the general populace and look with disdain on Christians who earnestly endeavor to follow their conscience in what they believe the Bible teaches. Since the origin of Protestantism in the sixteenth century, the attitude of the major churches has not changed.

There are two reasons for this. The first is the failure to comprehend fully the meaning of separation of church and state. Separation of church and state is endorsed up to a point and faithfully followed. But when it comes to practical implications in relation to war, the thinking suddenly stops short. The second reason relates to the area of eschatology. Because the principles of interpretation vary at this point, these major denominational bodies do not believe that Christ alone is the One who will establish a warless world when his kingdom is inaugurated on earth. Many people do not believe this is a possibility. It therefore falls upon the church and state together to maneuver in every possible way, even by means of war, to bring in an age of peace.

In support of this position they are able to marshall any number of problems calculated to destroy the validity of the doctrine of nonresistance. These appear to be absolutely insuperable. But they only seem that way. Where sufficient knowledge of Scripture is available along with a proper system of interpretation, these difficulties are greatly reduced. Three major objections to nonresistance include the military campaigns of Israel, the proclamations of Christ at various points and the place of the believer in relation to human government.

1. The first problem relates to the *practice of Israel* as recorded in the Old Testament. From the moment Israel became a distinct people with the call of Abraham and later when she was organized at Sinai into a nation, wars have characterized her history. As a result of the depredation of Sodom and the family of Lot, Abraham raided the retreating armies in the night, repossessed the goods that had been taken and released Lot (Gen. 14). Family difficulties almost erupted into armed strife between Jacob and Esau (Gen. 32—33:16). Israel suffered physical oppression in Egypt under hostile rulers (Ex. 1:8-14; 3:1-22). This led to flight from the land pursued by the army of Pharaoh (Ex. 13:17-22; 14:5-31). At Sinai, Israel was organized into a nation (Ex. 19—20). The arrangements of camp were made for the march through the wilderness and the fighting men were numbered (Num. 1—2). From that point on through the wilderness the Jews engaged in war against Amalek (Ex. 17:8-16), Sihon (Num. 21:12-32) and Og (Num. 21:33-35). Then there came the campaigns under Joshua and the judges for the conquest of the Promised Land (see the books of Joshua and Judges). The conquest of the land was not completed until David was crowned king and established Jerusalem as the capital of Israel (1 and 2 Samuel). After the division of the kingdom under Rehoboam both the northern and southern regions were constantly engaged in strife with hostile nations until

they were overrun by Assyria and Babylon.

It is difficult for Christian people to reconcile these wars, many of which were ordered by God, with the command not to resist evil by the use of physical force. If the people of God in the Old Testament dispensation were doing right when they engaged in carnal strife, then is it not proper for the people of God in the New Testament to engage in the same thing? This problem is very real, and it is useless to set it aside without some good reason. To relieve this paradox three things must be pointed out.

(a) Israel was a nation of this world, while the church is a spiritual organization not of this world. Israel was a nation just like any other, with the exception that Israel had been chosen by God. This people had distinct characteristics which differentiated them from all other people. They had a language, lived in a particular location and maintained a government with a capital city, a throne, a king and a royal family. In order to protect this nation, God permitted the use of physical force, for this was the only argument that would be understood by pagan peoples.

The church is not such a nation. Peter calls it "an holy nation" which has been "called . . . out of darkness into his marvellous light" (1 Pet. 2:9). The characteristics of this people are spiritual: its language is that of every land, its location is within every nation. It has no physical boundaries to maintain, no capital city to defend, no earthly throne to adore, no human monarch to protect. The Christian's native land is heaven (Phil. 3:20), and his holy majesty is the Lord Jesus Christ. Christians are pilgrims and strangers in this world, and therefore they do not possess any physical property in perpetuity. Their spiritual possessions cannot be taken by any show of physical force.

Since this difference between Israel and the church is so profound, it is easily understood why on the one hand Israel needed to protect her land with armies and carnal weapons, while on the other hand the church has no need for armies, lest she be found to be fighting against herself, for the church is in every land.

(b) Israel was not a regenerate people, while the true church is. "For what the law could not do, in that it was weak through the flesh, God sending his own Son in the likeness of sinful flesh, and for sin, condemned sin in the flesh: That the righteousness of the law might be fulfilled in us, who walk not after the flesh, but after the Spirit" (Rom. 8:3-4). The Israelites could not perform the righteousness of the law even though external pressure was brought to bear on them, for they walked after the flesh. Where unusual virtue was manifested by Old Testament saints, it was evident that the source was not the external pressure of the law, but the power of the Holy Spirit. The great masses of Israel lived on a very low moral plane as compared with the New Testament saints.

Inasmuch as Christians are expected to follow a much higher standard than the Old Testament Law, especially in the case of nonresistance, they have the resources of the Holy Spirit to enable them (1 Thess. 4:7-8). The Lord intended that this holy nation should display in the world the virtues of Christ (1 Pet. 2:9). Thus the call to nonresistance was given to blessed, born-again people (Mt. 5:3, 38-39) who will constitute the aristocracy of the coming kingdom. They ought to display today the virtues that will be fully realized when the kingdom is set up. Believers are the first fruits, the foreglimpse of the coming kingdom where all physical violence will be banished.

(c) Israel was a nation during the dispensation of the law, while the church is a spiritual entity existing during the dispensation of grace. Christ himself points to the past and the law which operated at that time and then with sovereign authority imposes a higher principle for the life of believers. "Ye have heard that it was said, An eye for an eye, and a tooth for a tooth" (Mt. 5:38 ASV). At this point Christ is citing Exodus 21:23-25, the principle for maintaining justice in Israel. Then without hesitation he raises the standard for believers to that of grace, "But I say unto you, Resist not him that is evil: but whosoever smiteth thee on thy right cheek, turn to him the other also" (Mt. 5:39 ASV).

This is the change made by Christ for his people during the dispensation of grace. The charge of inconsistency cannot be brought against Christ. He is the One who gave the Old Testament Law, and he has the sovereign right to change that standard when he deems it right and proper. The Old Testament Law was good in its place and served its purpose. But now a principle of conduct is imposed which supersedes the older and lower one, and which is to become the norm for a regenerate people living during the age of grace. This change from absolute justice and retaliation in kind to nonresistance does not mean that Christ is counseling believers to do nothing. If we read through to the end of Matthew 5, it becomes clear that an advance is to be made from justice to love. The believer is to go beyond the restraints of pure justice to the communication of positive benefit to the offender.

2. The next problem confronting the doctrine of nonresistance is inherent in *the proclamations of Christ* as recorded in the New Testament. Upon several occasions Christ made statements which seem to contradict his command on nonresistance. They are used by those who stand opposed to the doctrine. However, as in most cases when the immediate and larger context is examined, they fall easily into line with the general teaching of Christ on the use of physical force.

(a) Matthew 10:34 is the first passage that deserves attention. "Think not that I am come to send peace on earth: I came not to send peace, but a sword." At first glance this statement might appear to counsel division and the exercise of physical force. But the context makes it clear that Christ was calling for spiritual division. This would be effected by his person and his pronouncements. Some will believe in him; others will not. This sharp division among people produced by Christ is symbolized by the sword, but it is not the sword employed in physical force. The verses preceding and following clarify this (Mt. 10:25-42).

(b) Luke 22:35-38 constitutes the second passage. "And he said unto them, When I sent you without purse, and scrip, and shoes, lacked ye any thing? And they said, Nothing. Then said he unto them, But now, he that hath a purse, let him take it, and likewise his scrip: and he that hath no sword, let him sell his garment, and buy one." This passage of Scripture is admittedly difficult. And many commentators are uncertain of its precise meaning.

Some take this quite literally to mean that Jesus is counseling the use of physical force. Up to this point there has been divine provision and protection. But that period is now drawing to a close and wicked men are being permitted to use violence against Christ and his followers (v. 37). The disciples, too, took him quite literally, "And they said, Lord, behold, here are two swords. And he said unto them, It is enough" (v. 38).

But others feel that the reference to the time when they went without purse, scrip, shoes and sword is intended as a description of conditions that would characterize the coming rule of Messiah in his kingdom. But that is to be delayed, and wicked men are being permitted to have their day with its violence and deprivation. The disciples are therefore being forewarned that they must experience these conditions until the kingdom is established. Some measure of responsibility will rest on them for material provision and for self-protection.

Later, on the same occasion, when the vicious crowd had gathered to take Jesus, and Judas had betrayed Christ's identity to the enemy, the Bible tells us, "When they which were about him saw what would follow, they said unto him, Lord, shall we smite with the sword?" (Lk. 22:49). Before he could answer, "one of them smote the servant of the high priest, and cut off his right ear" (Lk. 22:50). "Then said Jesus unto him, Put up again thy sword into his place: for all they that take the sword shall perish with the sword" (Mt. 26:52). If in Luke 22 Christ was urging the disciples to use physical force in self-defense, then he has certainly reversed himself, for he is now admonishing just the opposite. To make amends for this impulsive and mistaken move on the part of Peter, the Lord graciously restored the ear of the servant.

Whatever our Lord meant by his statement about buying a sword, it certainly cannot be construed to mean that he is sanctioning war in any sense. If he meant self-defense in some limited sense, then it is to be explained in the light of other Scriptures instructing Christians on the use of physical force.

3. The final problem demanding attention is the proper *relation of believers to civil government*. Of all the objections this is perhaps the most difficult. It is especially difficult because believers naturally feel an obligation to their governments. And this is strengthened by the Scriptures which command Christians to respect, support and obey their rulers.

(a) The passage that is usually used to set forth the proper relation of believers to civil government is Romans 13:1-7. It is argued by some that verse 1 is sufficient to warrant obedience in military service. On the face of it and without regard to the context, this appears to be a legitimate interpretation. But in my judgment such a conclusion is based on a failure to note the primary intent of the passage.

The key to this passage is in verse 3: "For rulers are not a terror to good works, but to the evil." This means that the fundamental sense of organized government is to promote good and punish evil. For this reason believers ought to obey rulers where rulers are actually performing the function for which they were ordained of God. "Wilt thou then not be afraid of the power? do that which is good, and thou shalt have praise of the same: For he is the minister of God to thee for good" (13:3-4). Due to sinful human nature, rulers often fail to discharge this basic function of government. It is obvious that Paul is not arguing for Christians to do evil simply because it was commanded by the government.

This letter of Paul's was written in the days of Nero Caesar, a monster of iniquity and a sworn enemy of Christians. He is remembered to this day for his notorious deeds, and Paul was not in any sense condoning his wickedness. If Paul meant that believers should take up the sword (either in obedience to Caesar or against him), it is strange that he followed his counsel with the words, "Owe no man any thing, but to love one another" (13:8). The background of this exhortation in Romans (13:1-7) is the common knowledge among Christians of the low level of morality in the Roman government. The natural response was to rebel against such rulers. But this would have led them to exercise some form of physical violence. So Paul cautions them against the very thing that some interpreters would like to read into the text.

(b) Because true Christians bow in obedience to the Word of God in relation to human government, they are also conscious that there are times when they must obey the Word in matters contrary to government. This means that there is a higher law than that of humanity—that is the law of God. The believer should be subservient to political organizations in all things that are right. But even though God permits human governments to engage in war, God has limited the believer in this respect. He cannot engage in carnal strife which results in the taking of human life.

Christians are called to be separated from the things of this present evil world (Rom. 12:2), and this includes many things which are practiced by the citizens of the state. Physical violence is just one of those activities. In recognition of the prior claim of God on their lives, Christians must often bow to divine law in preference to the laws of civil government. Knowing that God has spoken clearly in his Word, the believer must obey him in refusing to take up arms for the purpose of taking human life. When Jewish authorities commanded the disciples to refrain from speaking of Christ, their answer was, "Whether it be right in the sight of God to hearken unto you more than unto God, judge ye. For we cannot but speak the things which we have seen and heard" (Acts 4:19-20). Later, to the same group when further threatened, they replied, "We ought to obey God rather than men" (Acts 5:29). This principle is sufficient authorization for refusing to bear arms.

This does not mean that the believer necessarily repudiates the authority of human government in relation to war. Believers may still serve the government in some capacity that is good, and thus fulfill their responsibilities to rulers. This may sound like pure casuistry to some because any service to the state aids in the taking of human life. This sort of reasoning is beside the point. In a wicked world it is necessary for every person to select the activities in which he or she is to be engaged. Christians must do this in all areas of life whether it be in times of peace or war. Since they cannot take life even in times of peace, they are under the same obligation during war.

A Christian Pacifist Response

Myron S. Augsburger

Dr. Hoyt has presented a practical biblical basis for the doctrine of nonresistance in war. Since this position is basically that held by my denomination, the Mennonite Church, my response is quite positive. Although I have written the chapter in this volume entitled "Christian Pacifism," my own position is better expressed by the term *nonresistance*. Nevertheless, there are several significant items in Hoyt's argument with which I take issue.

Present Vocation and Future Purpose

It is clear, as Hoyt points out, that nonresistance is a vocational calling. It is not a calling for the total society. It is rather a calling for the church. The church is not producing an ethic for the world, but an ethic for the regenerate, those who walk with Christ.

While we affirm that the total world stands under the moral demands of a sovereign God, it is also true that there are levels of commitment which mankind is willing to make. I believe that God meets man at those levels and holds him responsible for his commitment. The church is committed to the lordship of Jesus Christ and his kingdom and is thus responsible to operate "inside of the perfection of Christ," while the state operates "outside the perfection of Christ."[1] The vocational calling of the church is that of following the will of Jesus Christ as his disciples. As members of his kingdom we dedicate ourselves in a supreme loyalty to his lordship.

This is to say with Hoyt that the church exists in the world but is not of the world. The kingdom of which we are a part is "not of this world" (Jn. 18:36). "Our citizenship is in heaven" (Phil. 3:20 NIV), and we are responsible to live by the priorities of the kingdom of Christ. Hoyt is correct in making the concepts of separation and membership in the kingdom of heaven basic considerations for the doctrine of nonresistance.

It is important to see in the doctrine of nonresistance a positive dimension of love in action. For example, Jesus' teaching of turning the other cheek or going the second mile is not a surrender but is rather the Christian's strategy of operation. This is a working philosophy of life. This is not an escape from responsible action, but is an alternative to the patterns of this world. When Jesus answered the questions of the lawyer regarding the great commandment, he said we are to love God with our total being, that is, open our lives intimately to God in every area. Jesus could then say, "the second commandment is like this, to love your neighbor as yourself." When you open your life to God you must also open it to what God is doing in your neighbor, be he a friend or an enemy. Love is thus action; it is relating intimately and openly to others for their well-being and fulfillment.

Hoyt is to be commended for his use of the Sermon on the Mount. Jesus, as God's ultimate revelation, disclosed God's will in his total person: what he was, what he did and what he said. A hermeneutic which does not face the claims of his total teaching is inadequate. It is significant that with Hoyt's strong dispensational premillennial position he does not make the mistake that many dispensationalists have made, of relegating the Sermon on the Mount to the millennium. There is a refreshing approach to Scripture in Hoyt's treatise, seen in his recognition of the authority of the Sermon on the Mount as an essential part of Jesus' declarations of the will of God.

With respect to eschatology, it is important to recognize with Hoyt that kingdom fulfillment, the *telos* yet to come and the peaceful character of the kingdom, should already be influencing the lifestyle of the believer. However, one need not hold to a dispensational premillennialism to have the same beliefs in the personal, imminent return of Christ which then undergird the doctrine of nonresistance. For example, in my own brotherhood while many of us stand in the tradition of classical premillennialism, we have a major contingent which hold to amillennialism. But both are equally committed to peace and nonresistance and would see this as directly related to the meaning of the kingdom of Christ which is our ultimate loyalty now and will yet find its ultimate fulfillment in the future.

Undeveloped Views
Beyond this, there are several areas in which I feel Hoyt's essay needs further development. The first one has to do with the international nature of the present aspects of the kingdom of Christ. By this I mean that since our highest loyalty is to the kingdom of Christ, and since that kingdom is global, a Christian in one nation cannot honorably participate in war, which would mean taking the life of a Christian brother or sister in another nation. My point does not stop with this. Because of our evangelistic concern, we cannot take the life of another person for whom Christ died when we are committed to winning that person to the Lord. This is to say

that our separation from the world is not simply a negative separation, but a positive commitment to the community of Christ and to building the kingdom of Christ by evangelistic efforts. We are not simply refraining from participating in war, but are to risk our lives for the extension of the kingdom. I am quite certain that Hoyt supports this thesis, but I call attention to its importance in further developing the understanding of biblical nonresistance as a part of a total theology. The Christian church has a primary mission to penetrate other cultures with the gospel of Christ, and never to have the meaning of that gospel penetration altered by some national struggle for dominance or economic advantage.

Second, while Hoyt says that "nonresistance is not a part of some merely social program," I want to affirm that while we do not have a social gospel we do have a gospel-ethic which is social. The kingdom of Christ is constituted of persons. The kingdom becomes a new community within the social community. This community of believers and the concern for their well-being has social dimensions. In no way can the sharing of the gospel in the spirit of nonresistant love be authentic if it fails to enter into the social dimensions of this community. As I believe Carl F. H. Henry has said, "Christian experience is personal but never private." It is important to clarify that while we affirm the true Christian as not of this world, at the same time he or she is a participant in a Christian community within the world community. It is in this sense that the church is the visible expression of the new people of God. In fact, Paul says in Ephesians 3:10, that God is making known to the principalities and the powers *by the church* what his manifold purpose is all about!

Another area which needs more development in Hoyt's paper has to do with the relationship between the Testaments, a significant aspect of the hermeneutical issue. While the Bible is one unit, and one great covenant of grace, it is also an unfolding revelation in which God is continually saying more and more about himself. All the way through the Old Testament, God had something more to say about himself until he said it better in Jesus Christ. This means that the Incarnation is final, the full disclosure of God.

This has implications for the reading and interpretation of the Old Testament. It is correctly understood as God's Word when it is understood with the integrity of God's actions in his self-disclosure or revelation. God met men at levels which involved their practice of polygamy, the inequities between women and men, their limited understandings of his will for all peoples, and their limited understandings of tribal gods which prompted wars demonstrating that Yahweh is the greater God. It is important that we understand that God worked with and through a national Israel in the Old Testament, but that he now works through the church with a commission to "go . . . and make disciples of all nations" (Mt. 28:19). Similarly, the ultimate authority of Jesus Christ as the full will of God becomes the key through which we interpret the total Scripture. Christ is the Lord of Scripture, and the Incarnation becomes the final, ultimate expression of God's Word and will.

Model Citizens, But . . .

One further word may be shared on the significant point made regarding the separation between church and state. In reading Romans 13, it is important that this understanding enables us to recognize a very significant affirmation in this passage. When Paul writes, "the powers that be are ordained of God" (KJV), it does not necessarily follow that we thus obey the powers without question and are thereby obeying God. Rather, "the powers that be are ordained of God" means that God is still above the powers. He is the One who does the ordaining! Since God ordains government, we respect it fully as God's means of ordering society. But God is still above the powers, and there are times when we must say with the apostles, "we must obey God rather than man."

Christians should be excellent citizens in any state, respecting the government and praying for those in authority. But their citizenship in a given nation is second to their primary citizenship in the kingdom of Christ. They are good citizens because their contribution to national life will be with the integrity of Christian love, Christian morality and Christian service. Christians seek to enrich the lives of all with whom they associate, to extend the mission of Christian service into areas of need, and to exemplify by their own sacrifices the priorities of spiritual personhood over the sensual and material dimensions.

I cannot agree with Hoyt in his affirmation that Christians are free to serve their country in the army or under civilian direction in anything that is good. This position seems quite inconsistent with the basic affirmations of the article on nonresistance. Separation from the world's military program means a consistent, conscientious objection to identification with and support of the military enterprise. Noncombatant service still supports the function of war and at best only releases the individual from directly taking life, a legalistic distinction which misses the spirit of separation and discipleship.

The Christian is not only a conscience in society but an active agent of reconciliation between men and God and among people. To such Jesus says, "blessed are the meek: for they shall inherit the earth," meaning, if I may paraphrase, blessed are the meek for they are the ones who will fully enjoy what is intended for life on this earth. And again, "blessed are the peacemakers: for they shall be called the children of God," meaning, truly happy are those who live by peace for they are expressions of the very nature of God in contrast to the selfishness of man. As Paul writes in Romans 13:10, "love does no harm to its neighbor. Therefore love is the fulfillment of the law" (NIV).

A Just War
Response

Arthur F. Holmes

Nonresistance, pacifism and the just war theory share a
common concern about violence and war, and each seeks in
its distinctive way both to alleviate the suffering involved
and to work for peace. Within a Christian ethic, each seeks
to understand and obey what the Bible teaches. While I,
therefore, share Herman Hoyt's underlying concerns, the
question on which we differ is whether the Bible really does
teach what he proposes.

The view he takes of biblical nonresistance is that, while
the use of force and even of war may be legitimate for government, it is not legitimate for Christians. Separation from the
world means separation of church and state, and that means
church and state differ in both method and purpose, which
in turn precludes for the Christian any use of the force allowed to government. This is not a pacifist position which

rules war out altogether, since the state is allowed to use force.[2] Hoyt, therefore, sees a double standard, one for the Christian and one for governments.

In contrast to this, the just war theory holds to one standard for all people in all times and places. And, contrary to some other attitudes toward war to which Hoyt alludes, just war does not allow retaliation nor does it sanction every war and every military action. Rather, it is selective in allowing participation only in limited defensive wars. This fact becomes important in what follows.

Hoyt's case depends on his theological assumptions. Theology attempts to develop an overall conceptual scheme; but different theological constructs are possible, and evangelicalism is therefore theologically pluralistic. Just war theory's disagreement with Hoyt, then, is not settled by straightforward biblical texts whose meaning is obvious to all, about war. In fact, Hoyt does not discuss texts dealing directly with war. Rather the disagreement relates to different theological schemes. I, myself, think a somewhat Reformed theology does fuller justice to Scripture than the kind of theology he adopts and which shapes his understanding of crucial biblical texts. I shall focus on two of his assumptions.

Old and New Testaments

Hoyt is a dispensationalist, as he makes clear repeatedly in his essay. He believes that the two Testaments present different moral standards for different dispensations. Thus the law is "superseded" by grace—while the lex talionis with its "eye for an eye" (which he interprets as providing for retaliation) prevailed under the law, now it is replaced by loving nonresistance. Justice is therefore superseded by love.

This is not the place to discuss dispensationalism. But in rejecting the ethical discontinuity of the two Testaments and affirming one ethical standard for all peoples in all times and places, I make several observations.

First, the lex talionis (Ex. 21:24, etc.) says nothing about retaliation, with its vengeful spirit of hatred. Rather it speaks in context about criminal punishment, about retributive justice. Retribution, as distinct from retaliation, is society's means of maintaining a just and peaceful order and of punishing offenders. As Hoyt indeed acknowledges, the New Testament commits this function to government. But in reality no discontinuity exists between the principle of lex talionis in the Old Testament and the "sword" of Romans 13:4 in the New.

Furthermore, Jesus' words about loving one's enemies (Mt. 5:38-48) do not supersede civil justice. If that were the case, he would have been condemned as an anarchist! But he plainly says he came not to destroy the law but to fulfill it. And he drew the law of love directly from the Old Testament (compare Mt. 22:34-40; Deut. 6:1-5; Lev. 19:18, 33-34). Paul, too, tells us that love fulfills the law (Rom. 13:10). His term (anakephalupto) is a legal term used to mean summing up a case. A legal summation reaffirms in a nutshell what was argued in detail before. Thus love does not supersede the law's justice, but captures its spirit and intention: justice tempered by love.[3]

Finally, the lex talionis with its "eye for an eye" should be seen as both just and loving. In the ancient near East, grossly unjust and vastly disproportionate punishments were often the practice. The Old Testament Law insists on a proportionate response to evil and limits society's use of force. What applies to retributive justice must be applied elsewhere: only proportionate means and limited force are ever permissible—which is precisely what the just war view affirms.

Whether or not the Christian may have a role in retributive justice, moreover, depends on his or her relation to government, not on any ethical discontinuity between the two Testaments. It is plain that Old Testament believers had such a role. Affirming the ethical agreement of the Old and New Testaments, in accord with many theological traditions and indeed with some dispensationalists, I have to conclude that if Christians may not participate in the just use of limited force, the reason cannot be an ethical one. Old and New Testaments concur in mandating its use. Rather, if Christians are not to participate, the reason will be that they have another calling. This is a *vocational* difference and does not relate at all to the *ethics* of violence. Hoyt's position, apart from what he says about Old Testament morality, seems to be such a vocational view. But is that the clear teaching of the Bible?

Christians and Government

Related to his dispensationalism is Hoyt's "postponed kingdom theory." He says that God is now calling out an international aristocracy (that is, the church) for his kingdom, which was postponed because of Israel's unbelief. Consequently, Christ's kingdom is now a heavenly one: unrelated to earthly kingdoms. Again this is not the place to examine such a view,[4] but several observations will help focus the alternatives.

It is said that the Christian's main calling now is witness, and that military service would take too much time and effort. By the same token, of course, any engrossing occupation could take too much time—scientific research, business enterprise, teaching, even the noncombat military tasks which Hoyt's position allows. On the other hand, Christians in the military do in fact have an active witness, perhaps to people not otherwise reached. It is a well-known fact that soldiers wait a lot. But that fact and the alternative claim that they would have no time to witness are irrelevant to whether Christians may legitimately participate in the use of force. While witness may be a high priority, it is neither the Christian's only calling nor, if I understand Scripture correctly, is it our highest or all-inclusive duty. Our highest goal is to glorify God in all we do, to love God with all our being. Witness is one expression of this, but not the only one. People's gifts vary greatly in these regards.

Hoyt's case does not require what he says about witnessing. His main point seems at times to be that the two kingdoms are mutually exclusive. But he does not consistently make that claim, for he allows Christians to do some noncombat duties which still serve the purposes of earthly kingdoms. If the two were indeed mutually exclusive, no military service, no political service, no participation in the military-industrial complex and no participation in local government, criminal courts or police departments (to name just a few) would be permissible. A lesser claim must therefore be intended.

The same point must be made about the claim that Christ's kingdom is entirely otherworldly in its purpose and methods. Whether or not the Christian may use force, Christ has many purposes here on earth related to people's economic, emotional and physical needs, needs with which government also is in some ways concerned. One of God's means of meeting these needs is government, which has responsibility for distributive as well as retributive justice. And the New Testament makes plain that we are evaluated in terms of how faithfully we serve others in their varied needs. Saying that the purposes and methods of Christ's kingdom are not at all the purposes of this world is a serious overstatement. A lesser claim must be intended.

That lesser claim, stripped of overstatement, is simply that Christians should not use force. It is not that they should not contribute to any purpose of government or adopt any governmental methods. Christians may apparently serve many purposes here on earth: political, economic, social. Only force is specifically excluded (although Hoyt would doubtless agree to exclude other unethical or unbiblical practices as well).

My problem with this should now be plain. If force is

divinely entrusted to government and if the Christian should support and participate in just government in its rightful functions, then why not participate in legitimate governmental uses of force?

The biblical texts, as Hoyt points out, address believers as individuals rather than addressing nations or governments. Romans 12:9—13:14 is typical in this regard. The passage about government (13:1-7) is sandwiched between two discussions of the ethic of love. It does not directly address the war question, but it does grant to government the use of lethal force in maintaining civil peace and in criminal punishment. I am inclined to think that if such force may be used to resist criminal and violent attacks from within a country or community, by implication it may be used to resist criminal and violent attacks from without. But that is not now the point.

If Hoyt is right, a Christian may not serve as police officer, mayor or judge, or in any other force-executing role. At least, a Christian police officer must not use lethal weapons, and a Christian mayor should disarm his police. But Paul says no such thing. He instructs the Christian to pay the taxes that support governmental use (and abuse) of force. He condemns hatred (12:14), retaliation (12:17), a vengeful spirit (12:19) and over-reaction to evil (12:21). He expects Christians to go the second mile in their work (12:11), in loving their personal foes (12:14, 20) and in being peacemakers (12:18). But he does not rule out all limited and necessary uses of force on the part of any Christian who may be in government. And Paul had seen government officials become Christians. Moreover, since Old Testament believers participated in legal force, and Paul's teaching repeatedly builds on his Old Testament heritage, it seems that nonviolence is not in his purview—let alone total nonresistance.

Hoyt insists rightly that the church is not to use force. I heartily agree. But the individual Christian performs many divinely mandated tasks (economic, political, social and so on) which the church as such (considered as either the body of Christ or the local congregation) does not perform. The church does not perform any official political function, nor is it a profit-making economic enterprise. It does not vote, hold office or pay taxes. But the Christian does have a part in economic enterprises, pays taxes and has a political function. The church-state argument, therefore, does not rule out force any more than it rules out running for city council, voting in a presidential election or filling out an income-tax form.

Something is wrong, then, with the two kingdoms theory that underlies this view of the relation of Christians to government. The two are not mutually exclusive in all regards. The individual Christian does and should participate in both kingdoms. So what is the relation between them? I suggest that the kingdom of God is in principle all-inclusive, embracing the entire creation and including earthly government. In practice it does not yet command the loyalty of all creation, but even now God claims authority over governments as well as over families and businesses and churches. This view is more akin to that of Thomas Aquinas, that the eternal law of God embraces the whole creation and that it is manifest in natural law and even human law, as well as being more explictly revealed in Scripture to the church. In a different tradition, Abraham Kuyper, the Dutch theologian who became prime minister of the Netherlands, spoke of various "law spheres" in God's creation. Along similar lines, I suggest we must see God as the king of all kingdoms, who asserted his sovereignty throughout the Old Testament, consummately in Christ, and now through the work of Christians in government as well as in the church and elsewhere. What, then, is legitimate biblically for government is also legitimate for Christians who serve in government, or as the legal agents of government in military service. Our calling is to justice tempered by love. And this entails limited force in resisting violence.

Which Position?

Having said all this, we still have only discussed nonviolence, not nonresistance. It is a poor excuse that Hoyt himself led us to the issue of violence instead! I shall, therefore, add a few observations on nonresistance as such.

Should the church resist evil? Certainly, yes, but not by violent means. It should rather do so by its preaching and teaching, by ministering to the needs of those who might be tempted to erupt violently against society, by supporting just and compassionate government, by protesting today's social evils, injustices and violence.

Should individual Christians resist evil? Certainly, yes, for they participate in the church's resistance. And, yes, because they may participate in government's resistance to evil, perhaps by limited force. And, yes, because even as private individuals they may resist evil by legal and moral means, through community effort, education, the media and elected representatives in government, and by supporting arms reduction and progressive disarmament.

What then does nonresistance mean if it does not mean all of this? In Jesus' context (Mt. 5:39) it refers not to governments or churches but to individuals. It means that as an individual I do not take the law into my own hands. Instead of carrying out my own private scheme of retributive justice (lex talionis), I turn the cheek and go a second mile. It does not mean that justice no longer matters, that we have no stake and no part in law enforcement. Rather, nonresistance calls for love to replace hatred, for just and limited punishment to replace kangaroo courts, blood feuds or lynch mobs. In government, God has appointed us the means of justice. Individual vendettas are no substitute for legal punishment. Christian concern for the criminal will serve justice far better.

The example of Christ makes the point. In his sacrifice, God's justice and God's love met and both were satisfied. In the name of Christ, then, nonresistance cannot supersede justice with love; rather civil justice must be tempered by the victim's love for the offender. Biblical nonresistance therefore leaves retributive justice where God put the right to use force.

A Preventive War Response

Harold O. J. Brown

The key to Dr. Hoyt's appealing presentation of the concept of nonresistance is clearly his distinctively dispensational understanding of the church and his view of the implications of the spiritual (as distinct from constitutional) doctrine of the separation of church and state. It is important to distinguish Hoyt's view from the similarly named concept of Dr. Augsburger. In Augsburger's Anabaptist-Mennonite tradition, there is a tendency on the part of Christians to create separate communities, as isolated as possible from the world and its evil systems. This variety of separation may be symbolized by the Amish with their distinctively plain dress, buggies and oil lamps—cut off from the electric lines that bind worldly houses, businesses and institutions to one another. In the tradition of nonresistant dispensationalism, the separation of the believer from worldly society is more a matter of discrimination than of isolation. The Anabaptist wants a distinctive lifestyle for the Christian; the dispensationalist a distinctive mission. Thus Hoyt rejects participation in violence only for the Christian because the Christian has better things to do. It is for this reason rather than because violence is intrinsically evil that God has specifically forbidden believers—although not everyone—to engage in it. Violence is not so much wrong as someone else's business.

Church and State
Arthur Holmes's position as well as my own assumes that Christians and the church are parts of a larger community. We hold that as citizens, to some extent we must assume responsibility for and participate in what it does. Augsburger sees the Christian as a kind of "foreign national" in a nation at war—rather like Christians and Jews in countries being occupied by the Arabs during the early conquest of the declining Roman Empire. They were not even wanted as soldiers, at least not as long as they did not convert to Islam.

Hoyt, on the other hand, sees Christians as a kind of priestly caste among a secular people. We may characterize his position as "priestly pacifism," Augsburger's as "refugee pacifism." Thus, while Augsburger's case for state tolerance of Christian pacifism is predicated on the assumption that Christians are refugees or displaced persons passing through a nation at war, Hoyt seems to see them as a special caste, members of which do indeed share in secular society and can do more for it as noncombatants than they could as soldiers. Augsburger thus appears more modest. From the state he asks only tolerance in order to make his policy workable. Hoyt's approach seems to require that the state endorse and approve his view that the church is not merely separate from the state but of higher rank, performing as it were valuable state service according to another plan (or dispensation!). The state can be expected to approve Hoyt's position only if it is run by dispensationalists!

It is at this point that a fundamental difference in outlook between Hoyt on the one hand and nonpacifist Christians on the other becomes apparent. Those of us in the tradition of Reformation orthodoxy, especially its Reformed wing, accept the "political use of the Law"; that is, the doctrine that scriptural principles should guide not only the church, but also the secular state and civil society. This seems to be one implication of Paul's comment that the Law is (also) for the lawless (1 Tim. 1:8-10). Hoyt disagrees, saying, "The Scriptures were not in any sense directed toward unsaved men."

I believe that Hoyt and his tradition misunderstand the applicability of biblical principles of justice to worldly society. Although Hoyt urges attempts to propagate biblical teaching until all begin to observe it, he states that this condition will occur only upon the Lord's return. This seems to me to involve a measure of Christian irresponsibility. Surely if our evangelism meets with a measure of success in any society then Christians will have a voice in shaping its policies and directing its destinies. To the extent that Christians are few in number—as in the Ayatollah Khomieni's "Islamic republic"—the broader society will hardly require their help or solicit their counsel. But when Christians are numerous, as in the so-called Christian West, European Communist nations and parts of the Third World, society will demand more from them. They will not be left with the luxury of dispensational separation. For example, if all of America's Roman Catholics had sought noncombatant status in World War 2, the government would probably have revoked the relative consideration it granted conscientious objectors. Under such circumstances, if nonresistance is seen as a fundamental part of the Christian message, governments will cease to allow witnessing. And it is for the sake of witnessing that Hoyt says Christians are to shun military service. Incidentally, the noncombatant service he encourages Christians to perform would be as much a distraction from witnessing as would combat service. Many Christians have been effective witnesses as soldiers, not merely as medics.

A Spiritual Function

Inasmuch as Hoyt's concept of nonresistance is not a primary concept with him but derives from his understanding of the totally spiritual ministry of Christians during this present "parenthesis," my fundamental objection is directed at what seems to me to be an excessively spiritualized understanding of the church. His nonresistance is not a universally valid principle, but a select one for believers only. This is apparent from his rejection of philosophical and political pacifism and even of religious pacifism of the Mennonite variety. From this perspective it seems to make Christian observance elitist in a way that frustrates the ethical part of the Great Commission: "teaching them to observe all things whatsoever I have commanded you" (Mt. 28:20, KJV).

In addition, Hoyt is not antistate. He really seems to desire the preservation of our nation and social order. For this reason, he wants others—but not Christians—to defend it. This seems somewhat inconsistent. Those who approve capital punishment ought to be willing, in principle at least, to turn on the electricity. Hoyt claims a kind of priestly exemption peculiar to himself but not to society at large. But those who want to be defended should be willing to fight. Mennonites will not fight and do not want anyone else to fight either; this seems more consistent than the attitude that says, "I will not do it, but you go right ahead."

Hoyt is to be commended in his resolution to disobey man rather than God. But it is not apparent to me that God prohibits either capital punishment or just war, and therefore it is not self-evident that Christians should refuse to take part in them. Hoyt's position is truly that of a provisional, "interim" ethic to be followed by Christians pending the imminent return of Christ. I believe, however, that the doctrine of Christ's imminent return releases neither secular man nor Christians from accepting social responsibility in the interim (compare 2 Thess. 3:10-12).

If one believes, as the Anabaptists do, that war is never

right, then the Christian is being responsible by practicing pacifism. If one admits, as Hoyt does, that God permits human governments to go to war, then saying that Christians are to have no part in it is in effect shunning responsibility for what society is going to do anyway, with our taxes if not with our direct participation. This seems to be the equivalent of saying, as some do, "Abortion is killing, and I shall never participate, but I will not oppose those who do."

Of course what I call moral abdication Hoyt sees as obedience; this difference in views is attributable directly to his concept of the church as a gathered "aristocracy." This view fails more seriously than that of Mennonite pacifism, it seems to me, to do justice to the concept that the Christian is to be the salt of the earth (Mt. 5:13). We may call it a "little flock" view, one that presupposes that Christians will remain an insignificant minority that society can ignore. But when Christianity spreads, Hoyt's solution becomes inadequate.

II

Christian Pacifism

Christian Pacifism
Myron S. Augsburger

Jesus said, "Put your sword back in its place ... for all who draw the sword will die by the sword" (Mt. 26:52 NIV). And again, "But I say unto you, That ye resist not evil: but whosoever shall smite thee on thy right cheek, turn to him the other also" (Mt. 5:39 KJV). The Old Testament prophet said, "They will beat their swords into plowshares and their spears into pruning hooks" (Mic. 4:3 NIV), a prophecy fulfilled where the people take the way of Christ and his Spirit seriously. And the way of Christ is best found in his own words.

In Luke chapter six, we read, "But I say unto you which hear, Love your enemies, do good to them which hate you, Bless them that curse you, and pray for them which despitefully use you. And unto him that smiteth thee on the one cheek offer also the other; and him that taketh away thy cloak forbid not to take thy coat also. Give to every man that asketh of thee; and of him that taketh away thy goods ask them not again. And as ye would that men should do to you, do ye also to them likewise. For if ye love them which love you, what thank have ye? for sinners also love those that love them. And if ye do good to them which do good to you, what thank have ye? for sinners also do even the same. . . . But love ye your enemies, and do good, and lend, hoping for nothing again; and your reward shall be great, and ye shall be the children of the Highest; for he is kind unto the unthankful and to the evil. Be ye therefore merciful, as your Father also is merciful" (Lk. 6:27-36 KJV).

In John 18:36 Jesus says, "My kingdom is not of this world: if my kingdom were of this world, then would my servants fight, that I should not be delivered to the Jews" (KJV). Again in Matthew 5:9, Jesus said, "Blessed are the peacemakers: for they shall be called [known as] the children of God" (KJV).

These passages serve as a frame of reference for the discussion of nonresistance and pacifism. But much of how we interpret the Bible depends on how we come to it. Several years ago a man reacted to the reference in *Time* that I am a pacifist evangelist. He said he could not cooperate in an evangelistic crusade with me "because the Bible is a long way from a pacifist book; it is quite militaristic!" I say, it depends on how you read it.

First Things First

In any theological discussion it is necessary to state clearly the presuppositions by which or with which one is working. The following presuppositions are the basis for my position.

Theologically, God in grace is creating a people for himself, a people known as members of the kingdom of God. This kingdom is global, transnational and transcultural.

Christologically, the full revelation of God is Jesus Christ, who revealed the will of God in what he said, what he did and what he was. The New Testament presents Christ as nonresistant in his lifestyle.

Hermeneutically, the Bible as God's written Word is not a flat book. As an unfolding revelation it finds its culmination in Christ and the New Testament. One ought not to limit the New Testament teaching by the preliminary disclosures of the will of God in the Old Testament.

Sociopolitically, God is no longer working through a national Israel as his primary expression to the nations, but through the church which is to be present in every nation. This is an internal witness for godliness in every nation and a fellowship across nations as the kingdom of God.

Ecclesiastically, the church is a voluntary association of believers, a covenant community in which the kingdom of God has visibility, a minority in society always separate from the state (any state, recognizing that God has ordained government for the good of the people). The church is not coterminous with the state.

Soteriologically, salvation is by grace through faith, a faith which relates to or identifies with Christ who is the expression of grace or God's graciousness, this relationship being expressed in a discipleship of Christ more than in mystical religious sensations.

Ethically, the Christian lifestyle or ethics is related to Christology in the same way as salvation is related to Christology. Ethics is the expression of the new creation in Christ, and ethical norms are centered in the person and life of Christ himself.

Eschatologically, God's ultimate purpose is the completion of his kingdom and the vindication of salvation history in the ultimate reign of Christ, the present involvement in the kingdom of God being an introduction to its ultimate meaning. Whatever the nature of the millennium, this does not permit us to postpone, as though they are only applicable in a future millennium, the implications of the Sermon on the Mount and Jesus' ethical teachings.

These theological presuppositions are presented to enable readers to correctly understand the affirmations made in the following discussion. Without these you would judge my statements by your own presuppositions and not understand the arguments properly. It is my hope that sharing in this way will enhance dialog.

The discussion that follows takes as its foundation the explicit teachings of the New Testament rather than its silences. There are those who argue from silence—that since Jesus did not expressly condemn the centurian for being a soldier, it follows that military participation is right for the Christian. By the same logic one could argue for the practice of slavery, a stance taken earlier in American history. But the explicit teachings of the New Testament introduce a principle of love, a practice of respect for the ultimate worth of each individual, which when followed makes participation in both slavery and war antithetical.

The problem of the Christian and war is not one which can be viewed simply from the perspective of one's responsibility to his nation. We are now a global community in which we face the question of what violence does to all humanity. The increase of population, the problems of adequate food production and distribution, of meeting the basic necessities of life have made violence a way of life. Christians must have answers as they face problems of new dimensions in their relationship to other people around the world.

Furthermore, in viewing the question from the standpoint of our responsibility to our own nation, it appears impossible that there could be such a thing as a "just war" in a nuclear age with a world community. The arguments for a just war in history appear to be quite irrelevant in an age of modern, mechanized and nuclear warfare. But, theologically, the Christian must also face the meaning of the biblical affirmation, "as he is so are you in the world," or again the words of Jesus, "as the Father has sent me, even so send I you" (Jn. 20:21). Ours is a mission of announcing the good news of reconciliation to God, and through him to one another.

Minority Movement?

The problem of the Christian's relation to the state has always been a difficult one. It has divided the thinking of the church through the centuries. It now appears that the Holy Spirit has been teaching us something about history. Alan Walker, in his book, *Breakthrough: Rediscovery of the Holy Spirit*, suggests that history may be dated pre-Viet Nam and post-Viet Nam, and that nonresistant, redemptive love is the way of the future.[1] There is a growing consciousness in the church that war does not answer basic problems, that the Christian church exists in a hostile world, and that Christian discipleship is a movement of the minority who share the new life in Christ. This minority is to live now as members of another kingdom. Jesus said, "My kingdom is not of this world: if my kingdom were of this world, then would my servants fight, that I should not be delivered to the Jews, but now is my kingdom not from hence" (Jn. 18:36 KJV). When we accept the fact that the Christian church is a minority movement in a hostile world, then we can interpret the ethics of Christian discipleship for that minority. As Christians we are not here to provide an ethic for society or the state, but to clearly define an ethic for disciples of Jesus Christ.

In the American system of government it is difficult for this stance to be understood. We operate with the myth of being a Christian nation, and we seek to interpret for society an ethic that we can bless as Christians.[2] We need a new awareness of the pluralism of the New Testament, that the crucial issue is the difference between the church and the world, and that the church operates "within the perfection of Christ," while the world operates outside the perfection or will of Christ. Christians influence the state for good through Christian ethics and integrity, but they do not equate church and state. Only an in-depth understanding of this issue can save us from a cultural and a civil religion.

As one who believes in New Testament nonresistance,

or New Testament pacifism, it is important to me that this stance be clearly interpreted as an evangelical and biblical stance, not as the stance of humanistic or moralistic pacifism. Theologically, this position begins with the reality and priority of membership in the kingdom of Christ. This entails living by the way of love, a spirit of brotherhood and reverence for life. While brotherhood is an important concept, kingdom membership has first priority in New Testament nonresistance.

The question of the Christian's attitude toward war is viewed best by beginning with the New Testament, with Jesus Christ. This is to affirm that Jesus Christ brought the full meaning of God's will for us. All the way through the Old Testament God had something further to say about himself, about the will of God for humanity, and we see this fully in Jesus Christ. One can find numerous incidents in the Old Testament where Israel as the people of God was involved in war, enjoyed the blessing of God in victory and experienced defeat when out of favor with God. But a study of the context makes clear that God was meeting the Israelites where they were, demonstrating to people who worshiped their tribal gods that Jehovah, the God of Israel, was and is the true God. This is not to say that the full revelation of the will of Jehovah was then present. Rather, we see that there is progress in this revelation. Throughout the Old Testament God always had something further to say—until the New Testament. We read, "But when the fulness of the time was come, God sent forth his Son" (Gal. 4:4 KJV), and that "in these last days [God] has spoken to us by a Son, whom he appointed the heir of all things" (Heb. 1:2); that is, the One in whom the whole comes to its culmination. In Jesus' words, "Think not that I have come to abolish the law or the prophets; I have come not to abolish them but to fulfil them" (Mt. 5:17)—that is, to fill it full of meaning.

With this perspective we must recognize that peace is a holistic concept. Peace is not simply the absence of war. It is far more—it is positive, active peacemaking. The Hebrew word *shalom* contains in it the idea of wholeness or soundness.

To affirm that one is a member of the kingdom of Christ now means that loyalty to Christ and his kingdom transcends every other loyalty. This stance goes beyond nationalism and calls us to identify first of all with our fellow disciples, of whatever nation, as we serve Christ together. This is not a position which can be expected of the world nor asked of the government as such. The Christian respects rulers as God ordained them, to "protect the innocent and punish the evil doer." The Christian can only encourage the government to be the government and to let the church be the church. We ask the government to be secular and to let the church be free to do its work in society. The church enriches society by the many things it brings to it, and in its respect for government it does not subordinate itself to any particular social order but is in allegiance to its one Lord.

Properly read, Romans 13 is telling us that God ordains political institutions for ordering the society: But since God ordains the powers he remains above them. In that light our response on many occasions will be that as Christians, "we must obey God rather than men" (Acts 5:29). We cannot assume that since God ordains government we are always obeying God in our obedience to it. We are not to be lawbreakers, for Paul says that the authorities do "not bear the sword in vain" (Rom. 13:4). But we also cannot disobey a divine law to obey a contrary law by the government. The passage in Romans 13 calls us to be "subject to" the powers, but it does not use the term "obey." Our ultimate allegiance is to the God who ordains nations to function for order in society. Any serious attempt to resolve the question of a Christian's participation in war hinges significantly on this issue.

A Global Community
In his address to the Congress on Evangelism in Minneapo-

lis, Senator Mark Hatfield said,

> Communications have transformed our world into one
> neighborhood. Today more than ever before in history
> our neighbor includes anyone who lives with us on this
> globe. Consider the conditions of our world. Rather than
> looking at ourselves from a limited terrestial perspective,
> let us remove ourselves from the confines of our earthly
> environment. Picture our planet from outside of ourselves,
> from outer space. Look back on this blue, beautiful sphere
> floating through space and then consider that the inhab-
> itants of that planet spend fifteen times more money on
> creating weapons to destroy each other than on efforts to
> cooperate together for social and economic improvements.
> Yet 10,000 of its citizens die each day because they do not
> have enough to eat. Two out of every three children suffer
> from malnutrition; nevertheless the average diet in one
> portion of that globe contains about five times more pro-
> tein than the average diet of the remaining portion; 80%
> of that planet's wealth is controlled by only 20% of its in-
> habitants. The total wealth of those developed parts of this
> world is broken down to an average of $2,107 for each
> inhabitant, yet the total wealth of the remainder of the
> world equals only $182 for each person. This is the way
> we look from outside ourselves and our Creator views our
> world from that perspective.[3]

This quotation points out that grappling with the problem
of war is not an isolated issue but has to do with the problems
of the whole human community, involving race, poverty,
equal opportunity and the freedom for persons to be individuals. To face this matter honestly we must look at the larger
question of sin. As Samuel Shoemaker has said, "You do not
wait for a war to look at the problem of evil, war is simply
the problem of evil writ large."[4]

Closely associated with the preceding is the fact that war
is quite often for the protection of property. As Christians we
will respect the right of the government to declare war to

protect its own territory. But the Christian who is a conscientious objector to participation in war must be consistent with respect to his or her own attitude toward material things. The Christian must take seriously Jesus' teachings in the Sermon on the Mount that personality is more valuable than material goods and that we do not sacrifice life for the sake of goods (Lk. 6:29-35). This means that as Christians under a government which enables us to become wealthy we cannot ask the government to sacrifice people's lives in protecting our goods. The Christian attitude toward material possessions is not that of a legal right but that of responsibility, of a moral obligation to use the things he has acquired to help others.

In our society another question we must ask is, What are the guidelines for Christians participating in government? In an attempt to be consistent with the premise just stated, it would appear that Christians may serve in political positions so long as they do not try to create a state church. It is our responsibility as Christians to call the government to be secular and to respect the freedom of Christians to serve in loyalty to their own king. Christians will help interpret to others who hold political power why the Christian must constantly say, "Caesar is not lord; Jesus Christ is Lord." Thus, Christians should only serve at government levels where they can honestly carry out the functions of their office without compromising their fidelity to Jesus Christ as Lord. They should not consider holding positions where they could not both fulfill the obligations of the office and remain consistent with their membership in the kingdom of Christ. To fulfill their obligations and violate their commitment to Christ would be wrong. Likewise, to live by their convictions and not fulfill the functions of their office with respect to the society which creates the office would also be wrong. The Christian in a political position serves the goal of effective government just like a secular person, but the Christian is a witness to the higher values of Jesus Christ. Christians ought never to use a powerful government position as a means to achieve Christ's goals for humanity. For the Christian, the desire to "rule" is always wrong; our stance is one of serving. This awareness will keep us from the struggle for power, a struggle which Malcolm Muggeridge has called "a pornography of the will."[5]

One who accepts this stance—that New Testament non-resistance is the claim of Christ upon his disciples as an expression of the reality of his kingdom—will also follow other evangelical premises of faithfulness to Christ. For example, can one participate in war and take the life of a person for whom Christ died when our basic mission as Christians is to win that person to become a brother or sister in the Lord? Or, since the kingdom of God is global and transcends every national, racial and cultural distinction, when one's country is at war with another country can Christians participate knowing that by so doing they may be at war with persons who claim to worship and follow the same Lord?

To go back to the early church itself, according to several writers of history, there was in the church a significant percentage who renounced conflict and everything that produced war. The one thing Christians were armed with was love. E. Stanley Jones wrote that we search in vain during the early years of church history to find Christian people engaged in warfare. He states that Christians did not become soldiers. If they were in the army when converted, they resigned. Jones describes the early believers as saying, "we will match our power to suffer against your ability to inflict suffering, we will wear you down by our spirit, by soul force against physical force, by going the second mile, by turning the other cheek," until Rome finally stopped torturing Christians.[6] That perspective on history underscores the New Testament emphasis that we go out not by force but by love; we seek to make our world an understanding community.

This disdain of military service held true until the period

of Marcus Aurelius, emperor of Rome until about A.D. 180. After Constantine's time, who from our perspective instituted a "fallen church" of which everyone was forced to be a member, there were many "Christian" soldiers.

In our own era, Martin Luther King, Jr. brought into the American scene a new synthesis. It was not novel in terms of what he emphasized from the New Testament, but because he borrowed from Ghandi's philosophy. He created a new synthesis by enhancing New Testament nonviolence with Ghandi's strategy of nonviolent resistance and applying these to the nineteenth-century liberal idea of "the kingdom of God in America." What King did was to confront society with this new dimension, and it shook the country to its roots.

King's philosophy is expressed in five points: (1) Nonviolent resistance is not a method for cowards. It takes more strength to stand for love than to strike back. (2) Such resistance does not seek to defeat or humiliate the opponent, but to win friendship and understanding. (3) The attack is directed against forces of evil rather than against the people doing the evil. (4) Nonviolent resistance is a willingness to accept suffering without retaliation, to accept blows from the opponent without striking back. (5) This resistance avoids not only external physical force, but also internal violence of spirit.[7]

On the premise that we cannot kill people for whom Christ died, John Howard Yoder emphasizes in his significant writings on pacifism that the cross has made a difference.[8] Christ has come into the world to redeem all people and has acted for the sake of every person on the globe. We cannot kill a person for whom he died and rob him or her of the privilege of knowing the fullness of life that Jesus Christ offers. This calls us to express a pacifist position not by a negative but a positive stance. Ours is to be an active penetration into society with the redeeming love of God. Above everything else, we want our fellow men to become our brothers in Christ.

When Jesus stated that the first commandment is to love God and that the second is just like it (to love your neighbor as yourself), he was asking that we bring to bear on the life of our neighbor that which we find most important in our own relationship with God.

The early church father Tertullian expresses this same concern in his teaching against war; that is, that we cannot take the life of a person God purposes to redeem. Our task is instead to bring the meaning of Christian grace and brotherhood into all of life. Humanity chooses force; Jesus Christ has come to say there is a better way! For two thousand years the professing church has rather consistently rejected Jesus' way of love and has turned to force, until now in the modern world God has let humanity discover atomic energy. It is as though he says, "You have put your faith in force, so I am going to let you see into the heart of an atom and see that the only end of this course is destruction. . . . They that take the sword shall perish with the sword." On the other hand, it is true that wherever the gospel of Jesus Christ has been taken seriously in the world, believers have literally beaten their swords into plowshares and their spears into pruning hooks!

From an evangelical perspective it may be said that wherever a Christian participates in war he has abdicated his responsibility to the greater calling of missions and evangelism. The way for Christians to change the world is by sharing the love of Christ and the good news of the gospel rather than to think we can stop anti-God movements by force. Jesus made this point ultimately in the Garden of Gethsemane and on Calvary's cross. As Christians, our answer to the violence in the world is simply that we don't have to live; we can die. This is the ultimate testimony of our belief in the kingdom of Christ and the resurrection. It is this same conviction which has motivated many people to go into unknown or violent areas of the world from which they may never return.

A Matter of Obedience

Another evangelical premise that leads to a nonresistant view is that we regard Christ's Word in the Scripture as final. Having said that the New Testament is a culmination of God's will known in Christ, then it follows that his Word is final. He corrects the understanding of the old "eye for an eye, tooth for a tooth" attitude. God gave that position to limit violence, that is, only an eye for an eye. But now he declares that we are to love our enemies. He tells us that we will be better for the loving. We will be better people, better neighbors, better friends when we live by love. In answer to the question of whether this will work in our society, he showed us that we do not have to live; we can die. In dying we may sometimes do more for enriching the world than we would have done by living. We cannot answer the question of war on the basis of whether or not someone must suffer. Of course they will, one way or another. The question is, Which kind of suffering will we choose—that imposed by war or the suffering which comes because of love?

When troops move to take a beachhead, they do so with the conscious plan that they will sacrifice thousands of men. What if the Christian church moved into the world with the same conviction? What if we had a conscious plan to follow even though it might cost many lives? While there are conditioning factors to this comparison, it would appear that before the Christian church justifies giving the lives of so many of its people in military involvement it should look at the greater sin of being unwilling to sacrifice lives of affluent ease for the cause of building the kingdom of Christ.

Jesus says, "Put up your sword," and history has proven that warlike nations perish. When people take the course of violence, they suffer the consequences. This is seen in the image that America is creating in the world today. We are no longer looked on as a friendly, gracious people. We are looked at in terms of power. We have established a pattern of using force to answer the world's problems.

Whose Citizen?

As Christians we regard membership in the kingdom of
Christ as our primary loyalty. Such an outlook is even
more basic to the New Testament than the principle of love.
Jesus himself said that he came to introduce another kingdom. Its spirit is one of love, but its platform of operation
is loyalty to another Lord, an authority separate from any
earthly power. This premise, which says that our primary
loyalty is to the kingdom of heaven, underscores the fact that
we answer first of all to Jesus Christ and his mandate alone.

This is true with respect to any given culture or nation in
which a Christian lives. A believer will seek to be a good
citizen, but with the awareness that there are many valid
contributions Christians can make for the good of their fellow citizens when they give of themselves in a positive way.
This should not be overlooked by those who imply that if
one does not participate in military action he or she is not
contributing to the nation. We carry an ethical responsibility
to demonstrate that the position of conscientious objection to
war is not something that you "turn on" during a war, as
though this is the way to avoid several years of military service. Nonviolence is a total way of life. It means that we give
ourselves in service to others. We are not to build status as
people who give themselves to a materialistic power struggle.

Some readers may ask, Does Augsburger not understand
that God used war in the Old Testament and blessed it? The
answer is simply yes, this is well understood, but interpreted in relation to the "unfolding revelation" in which God
moved men to higher levels of understanding of his will.
I say this with a deep conviction in the full inspiration of
Scripture. There are no contradictions of meaning in the
Bible. But I am also convinced that the Bible is not a flat book.
It is rather an unfolding revelation of God's will in Jesus
Christ. God is no longer using a nation to achieve his pur-
pose, but rather using the fellowship of believers, the church

of the reborn. Instead of using a nation, Jesus Christ has given us the Great Commission to go into all the world and make disciples of all nations. This is our mission: discipling people to become members of the kingdom of Christ, not helping to justify participation in war. David Ben Gurion's question still confronts the Christian church: "When are you Christians going to begin working for peace?"

The love that is basic to the Christian's relationships with others is a volitional as well as emotional love. This means that we as Christians must find the way to build bridges of understanding. One problem that we face is to discern the course of love. A further problem is how to express that love. Certainly this involves more than merely talking about the problems. Many young people have given themselves through alternate service to the promotion of brotherhood, of peace and of understanding through rehabilitation and aid for those who are suffering. Nonresisters are not simply protesters.

Service in love must become a part of our whole philosophy of life. Our choice of vocation as well as our other involvements should be an expression and extension of the love of Jesus Christ. To open one's life to another makes the question of peace inescapable. We must ask what we can do with respect to Cambodia, Israel, Egypt, the Palestinians, South Africa and South America. Instead of waiting for a catastrophy to happen, we should be penetrating our world with acts of love to help alleviate its ills.

As Christians we believe in the infinite value of every human life. As Kant said, we should treat each person as an end in himself, not as a means to an end. We thus oppose any kind of revolutionary tactic which sacrifices persons for the sake of goals. Rather, from our Christian perspective we believe that deterioration occurs when people follow a course of violence as an answer to the world's ills. Believing in the sanctity of human life, we cannot be involved in anything, whether it is social injustice, violence, war or poverty, which interrupts a person's opportunities for a full life.

Committing oneself in ultimate loyalty to Jesus Christ means becoming a conscience to society, where that society operates beneath the level of the will of God. As members of the kingdom of heaven, obedience to Christ is the basic aspect of our approach to the question of war.

The story of the good Samaritan highlights what it means to be a member of the kingdom of heaven. The interesting thing in this account is that it stands in judgment on everyone. The story of the good Samaritan addresses the priest and the Levite as churchmen, and then shows that while these people could sit and talk about issues, when it came to concrete experience, they could not walk across the road to help a man who had been robbed and beaten. One of the sad facts about our life as a church in American society is that we can often talk about loving man in general, but not do anything about loving individuals. We can love people across the ocean and not walk across the street to help someone in need. The real consistency of our objection to war has to do with more than simply being opposed to war.

Every good humanitarian will say that war is sin and that conflict should cease. But there are those who believe that the world is sinful, and we cannot escape war. I wrote a paper on Charles Clayton Morrison's views as editor of *The Christian Century* during World War 2. I read everything he wrote, watching this man change to a pacifist position and then give it up because he felt war was hell, and in hell there are no morals. So, all one could do was get it over with (get rid of Hitler) and allow life to start again. That is the process a person goes through when he follows humanitarianism and does not keep in the forefront the demands of Jesus Christ which are much higher than either nationalistic or humanitarian ideals.

There are at least three other views of war held by the modern Christian church. One is that war is the lesser of two evils, and we cannot avoid it as an option. Another is that we turn to war only as a last resort. And another is that the Christian should be able to move beyond hate and kill in love. But from my perspective the issue is not answered by any of these, rather it is to be faced by the people of God on the basis of the character of his kingdom.

With the horror of Hitler's gas chambers, the tragedies of Viet Nam, the assassination of national leaders and the violence rampant in American society, it is imperative that the Christian church give a more clear witness to peace. My intent here is to call for a Christian conscience to counteract violence by positive actions of love and thereby to promote peace in our society and in the world. Such activity is not a neutralizing of relationships, but an active expression of the love of Christ which treats every person as having ultimate worth.

In conclusion, I note again Paul's statement in Romans which admonishes Christians to respect government and pay its dues: "Owe no one anything, except to love one another; for he who loves his neighbor has fulfilled the law" (13:8). Believers are to "repay no one evil for evil, but take thought for what is noble in the sight of all" (Rom. 12:17). And, in the words of Jesus, to render to Caesar only what is Caesar's and render to God what is God's (Mt. 22:21).

A Nonresistant Response

Herman A. Hoyt

From the opening word of this article to its close, the reader is increasingly convinced of Dr. Augsburger's absolute sincerity. He writes as one who is completely involved in the program he is advocating. In his estimation no other position can be substantiated on the basis of the Scriptures. To him, the positive promotion of love by the Christian in a warring world is the only open path. It is therefore not surprising that the essay begins with a series of quotations from the Scriptures. Five passages come from the New Testament and in each case, from the words of the Lord Jesus (Mt. 5:9, 39; 26:52; Lk. 6:27-36; Jn. 18:36); one passage is cited from the Old Testament (Mic. 4:3). In character with the theme, the major emphasis must be on the New Testament. But this emphasis is also in agreement with the writer's hermeneutic. As the author declares, the passages already cited provide the framework for the discussion of nonresistance and pacifism.

Reading between the Lines

Presuppositions underlie every discussion, and here they are absolutely essential to the understanding of the direction in which the writer is moving. So that the reader may be prepared, Augsburger states his position at the very outset. But even this preliminary declaration of presuppositions does not adequately divulge everything that is necessary for evaluating the article's conclusions.

The theological presupposition cannot be completely understood by itself. It must be weighed over against the hermeneutic set forth later. It is true that God in his grace is creating a people for himself, a people known as members of the kingdom of God, a kingdom that insofar as the church is concerned is global, transnational and transcultural. But this does not make the church the kingdom of God, nor does this limit the members of the kingdom to the church. There will be other companies of saved people who will someday occupy a place in the kingdom.

As for the Christological presupposition, it is true that Christ is the perfect revelation of God. But there is also a revelation of God in the Scriptures and in nature and in the life and experience of God's people. Christ revealed the will of God in what he said, did and was. He was nonresistant in lifestyle, and New Testament writers admonish believers to "follow his steps" (1 Pet. 2:21). But not everything he said and did is to be understood by this injunction. There were times when Christ was subservient to the state (Mt. 17:24-27), even a foreign government in control over Israel.

As for the hermeneutic, it is true that the Bible is not a flat book in that its revelation is complete at every point in its disclosure. Progressive revelation characterizes its movement, and it does find culmination in Christ. But this does not mean that New Testament revelation invalidates, supplants or excludes the revelation of the Old Testament. The New Testament does have a special message for the church, and that is pertinent to the discussion at hand. But there is

a vast portion of the Old Testament that is yet to be fulfilled
in relation to other companies of saved people, as for instance, the nation of Israel and also the gentile nations.

While it is true that God is not *now* working through a
national Israel, it is not true that God is *no longer* working
through this people. His will today is being wrought through
the church, but his program for the future includes Israel
as a nation (Acts 15:13-18). His chosen people are not cast
off and therefore expendable (Rom. 11:1-2, 26). It is quite
true, however, that Christians inhabit every nation and are
responsible to give a witness for godliness in every nation.
Christians constitute a sociopolitical fellowship that is vital,
for the Spirit of God indwells each one (1 Cor. 3:16-17; 6:19-
20).

When appraising the ecclesiastical presupposition one
must be careful to understand that the church is a minority
in society, separate from the state, though living in the state.
It is a mystical body not necessarily coextensive with the
organized local assemblies of Christians. But true Christians, who constitute this mystical body, give visible witness
to the work of Christ in the world.

On the soteriological level, salvation is by grace through
faith in Christ. This faith not only appropriates the life of
Christ, but also identifies the believer with Christ. This
brings the believer into a position of discipleship. In this
respect he or she is taught of Christ and is obligated to follow Christ's teaching. While religious sensations may be
involved, this relationship does not arise out of mystical experiences. It is the life of Christ imparted by the Holy Spirit.

In the ethical realm, lifestyle and conduct are an expression of the indwelling Christ (Phil. 1:21; 2:12-13). As Christ
deported himself in society, he thus provided a model and
example for the believer. Augsburger is correct in declaring
that inasmuch as salvation is the impartation of the life of
Christ to the believer, it is logical and natural for the out-
working of that salvation to result in conformity to the life

of Christ on earth. There is no reason to believe that Christian ethics should differ from the ethics of Christ.

When it comes to the eschatological presupposition, there are many who will differ radically with Augsburger. But it is my opinion that Augsburger is right when he asserts that "God's ultimate purpose is the completion of his kingdom and the vindication of salvation history in the ultimate reign of Christ." I also believe that redemptive history extends through the millennium, when it will be brought to completion (1 Cor. 15:24-28). Nevertheless, the present involvement in the church constitutes an important part in which God is preparing an aristocracy for the kingdom and the eternal state. Since that is true, there are ethical teachings in the Sermon on the Mount, later emphasized in the New Testament Epistles, that are applicable right now.

A Look at the Argument

It sounds plausible that we should argue from the statements of the New Testament and not from its silences. While this is generally true, and the instance cited (slavery) largely validates this point, it should also be realized that statements have implications that are not explicitly stated in the New Testament. This is tacitly admitted when the author says, "the Christian's relation to the state has always been a difficult one." It has divided the church through centuries, and it still does. It separates even those who are committed to the doctrine of New Testament nonresistance, such as Augsburger and myself.

Christians are not only members of an earthly nation with fixed boundaries, they are also members of a global community without boundaries. Therefore, Augsburger is correct when he states that any discussion of this problem solely from the perspective of responsibility to an earthly nation is bound to be a discussion in the realm of low visibility. All humanity is affected by war, and this has been emphasized in our day by two world wars. The vast increase in population, the prodigious problem of food production and distribution and the devastating methods for mass extermination, make a "just war" impossible.

No matter how logically one may reason toward solution on the human and natural level, Christians cannot ignore the sovereign Lord and his directives. Christians live in the world but have been chosen out of the world and are duty-bound to separate themselves from this world. Surely this extends to the exercise of violence, whether personally or militarily. Augsburger is right in asserting that the believer's mission in this world is one of love and good will. He or she is especially commissioned as an ambassador of reconciliation to a lost world (2 Cor. 5:17-21).

Though the author makes reference to Alan Walker's book *Breakthrough: Rediscovery of the Holy Spirit*, that history may be dated pre-Viet Nam in relation to nonresistance. I was also led to think along these lines as a result of developments within U.S. soldiery. However, let it never be forgotten that the moment danger assails our own boundaries, homes and loved ones, there will be a radical revolution in such thinking, and war mania will sweep the land again. In the face of this possibility, Christians will be forced to reassess their relationship to the Lord Jesus Christ and the alternatives of participation or nonparticipation in war.

Augsburger insists on some absolute lines of cleavage in thinking if the position of nonresistance is to be understood. It must start with the fact that nonresistance is evangelical and biblical, not humanistic and moralistic. There is only one place to discover this position, and that is in the Bible. There it will be discovered that it is evangelical in nature. It is definitely a part of the good news of salvation for mankind. Nothing in humanistic philosophy or human moralizing quite approximates this view of things. There are two levels of thinking which mutually exclude one another. The higher can evaluate the thinking on the earthly and natural level, and must of necessity reject it as unchristian and unbiblical. But the lower cannot evaluate the higher, for "the natural man receiveth not the things of the Spirit of God: for they are foolishness unto him: neither can he know them, because they are spiritually discerned" (1 Cor. 2:14 KJV).

It is therefore incumbent upon the person who desires to understand the position of nonresistance to become a child of God and by so doing to become in reality and priority a member of the true church. As Augsburger puts it, one then becomes a member of the kingdom of God, where spiritual brotherhood prevails and the rule of life is the law of love (Lk. 6:27-35). This will produce a new evaluation and reverence for life (Gen. 9:6; Jas. 3:9; 1 Cor. 11:7; Acts 17:28; 1 Jn. 4:20). Since men were created in the image of God, that image, though marred by sin, has such high value that Christ performed a work at Calvary to restore it (Gal. 4:4-5). Being redeemed from the law and the old life, the believer ought never to be entangled again in that old life (Gal. 5:1). He or she ought rather to use the new liberty for an expression of love on behalf of others (Gal. 5:13-14).

The author points out that Christians respect government for the purpose for which God ordained it, namely, to protect the innocent and punish the evil doer (Rom. 13:1-7). It is not within the province of human government to compel the doing of evil, only good. Whenever the government calls for activities that believers are forbidden by divine authority to perform, then they must bow to the higher power (Acts 5:29). This does not mean insubordination to human government. It merely means that human government has introduced a demand contrary to divine intention, and the Christian cannot conscientiously obey and be true to the sovereign authority of Christ (Acts 4:19-20).

Augsburger supports clearly the fact that being a child of God and under the law to Christ makes it imperative that the law of love be the controlling principle in every facet of life. If believers serve in government, it must be for that which is good: to preserve the life of the people for whom

Christ died; to protect the saved person who serves in a hostile army; to bind up the wounds of those who have been ravaged by war; to spare the innocent in civilian society; to promote the welfare of the human community; to use every potential of life in an unselfish devotion to the good of humanity and the glory of God.

"Every good humanitarian will say that war is sin, and that conflict should cease." To this statement by Augsburger there are three views taken in the modern church. One viewpoint holds that the proper response is to take the lesser of two evils. In the face of greater evils from tyrants and wicked nations, war to correct this situation, or at least to arrest it, is to be preferred. Another widely held position is that we turn to war as a last resort. There is a third view, namely that of confronting evil with the law of love.

It is difficult to analyze the concluding remarks. Does Augsburger intend to suggest that the law of love, which he has so consistently supported and which belongs to the Christian and the church, shall now be applied to nations? If so, this is to suggest that the government is not permitted of God to use force when necessary to carry out its mandate. Surely, he cannot mean that. Then perhaps he is suggesting that Christians must be completely separated from war in all of its ramifications. If that is his meaning, then I wonder how Christians can do this except by departure from the world. They must pay taxes. They must be engaged in some enterprise which makes its contribution to the war effort. They dare not stand up in the face of these responsibilities and refuse. Of course, they can die.

It would seem there is some middle-of-the-road position which neither compromises our responsibility to human government on the one hand, nor constitutes dereliction of commitment to Christ on the other. I trust that that is the import of this fine discussion on the Christian and his relation to war.

A Just War
Response

Arthur F. Holmes

Myron Augsburger's pacifism resembles the nonresistance view set forth by Herman Hoyt, and as a result much of what I would say has already been said in response to Hoyt. This pertains especially to the relation of Christians to government and the relation of the Old and New Testaments. While Augsburger does not build his case on dispensationalism, and while I agree with him that the Bible is not a "flat" book, yet he still finds ethical discontinuity where I do not. In my view, God holds people of all times and places accountable to one and the same moral law (Rom. 1—3). A Christian may be called to go a second mile in love, but grace neither supersedes nor abrogates the morality that is universally binding.

I heartily agree with Augsburger's repudiation of nuclear war: it is as unthinkable for the just war theory as for pacifism. I agree that war does not solve the larger problems, but often creates new ones. I agree that our ethical obligation

transcends any nationalism and all obligation to governments. However, I question whether wars are (or should be)
fought to defend *property,* and I am surprised he does not
address the right of governments to use force to defend
innocent *lives* against aggression. That, it seems to me, is
closer to the heart of the question. But in any case we are
in agreement that we should seek peace, in the large *shalom*
sense of a just and loving peace in and through all we do. The
just war theory has always insisted that the only proper end
in going to war is to secure a just peace for all involved. In
that regard, I can make common cause with the Christian
pacifist. My disagreements are twofold.

Approach to Social Evils
Both Augsburger and I are desparately concerned for peace.
The disagreement is over what we can do, while seeking
peace, to limit war. I think that biblically more is required
of us than bearing witness (by political process as well as
otherwise) to a better way.

Consider how social evils are dealt with in the sweep of
biblical revelation. First, the law limits the evils involved
by insisting on just and equal treatment with compassion.
The kings were expected to uphold both the letter and intent
of the law, and the preaching of the prophets holds all people
accountable. In the pedagogical function of law, justice and
love are at work. Jesus too points back to these beginnings.

Gradually grace (already operative in the Old Testament
but more fully revealed in the New) changes people, and
through them the institutions they shape are changed, in
preparation for the coming kingdom.

This pattern can be traced in Scripture with regard to both
divorce and slavery. From the beginning, marriage was intended to be lifelong. Human hardheartedness sometimes
prevents this; marriages tragically break down. Moses therefore allowed divorce and provided legislation to protect
those who might otherwise be unjustly treated (Deut. 24:1-4;

Mt. 19:3-9). The prophets repeatedly condemned adultery and other violations of marriage. Jesus reaffirmed the original lifelong intent, and the New Testament makes clear that God's grace will nurture the love and loyalty that can make and keep marriage whole.

In regard to slavery, the Old Testament Law provided what in those days were extremely humane regulations to protect the rights of slaves. Their lives were safeguarded: they could not be mistreated with impunity. In this regard, they had the same rights as free men. In addition, Israelite slaves were to be freed in the course of time. Attitudes cultivated in this way are clearly meant to erode the whole institution of slavery. Paul's teaching on love and mutual service between slaves and master is even more explicit. His words to Philemon, the master of a runaway slave, cut any residual ground of unconcern from beneath the whole practice: "Receive that slave as a brother!"

This seems to be the biblical pattern: law and grace work together educationally and redemptively, limiting evil, changing attitudes, transforming social practices and even institutions. The same pattern, I suggest, is applicable to the evil of war and violence. Just, equitable and compassionate limitations are only a beginning, but the kind of a starter that the law taught (Deut. 20:10-20; Ex. 21:24), that prophets preached (for example, Amos 1—2 and that the New Testament reaffirms in its teaching on government (Rom. 13:1-4; 1 Pet. 2:13-14).

Obviously, the ideal is that all violence should cease; and I have pointed out elsewhere in this volume that if war were only defensive, as the just war theory requires, then all war would cease. But meanwhile, just laws intended to reduce violence remain essential in any society. The just war theory inculcates both peace-loving attitudes and limits to violence. To an extent, its rules have shaped international law, the Geneva Convention and even army regulations. The limitations it asks are not an alternative to the quest for peace, but a step in that direction. Yet in the light of the biblical pattern of the law, prophets and grace together combating evil, and in view of the biblical teaching on government, I take it to be the kind of step we still sadly need.

The Value of Human Life

Both Augsburger and Hoyt speak as if human life under all circumstances is utterly sacrosanct. Every life, we are told, is "of infinite worth." This I think is mistaken. If it were the case, then nothing would be worth risking one's life for, or dying for—whether violently or by sheer exhaustion. Nothing would have warranted the death of Christ, and his giving his life would have been a sin. Perhaps the human person with his eternal destiny is utterly sacrosanct, but not physical, biological existence. Yet even there I hesitate, for theism insists that *only God is of infinite worth*. Every creature has worth that is limited by God's infinite worth and is as contingent on God as is one's very existence.

Two further incongruities would be involved. First, if each human life is of infinite worth, then God's mandate to governments to allow the use of force would violate that worth. God would be contradicting himself. Second, if each human life is of infinite worth, then the Old Testament commandment against killing would be utterly exceptionless. But it is not; the context plainly allows capital punishment. Whatever one thinks of that for today, it would contradict the concept of the infinite worth of a life.

As for the argument that killing prevents the victim's accepting God's mercy, the same plea could be leveled against giving the sword to governments, against the Old Testament uses of divinely commissioned force, and against God himself for allowing human mortality at all. Even more tragic is the fact that in any case not all will be saved.

The point about the sanctity of life is that no God-given rights are absolute, unconditional or without exception. The very nature of legal punishment (ordained by God) is that it abrogates some right to property (fines) or liberty (imprisonment) or even to life itself. The call to love one's enemies does not change the picture for, as I pointed out in response to Hoyt, the law of love embraces rather than excludes retributive justice.

All that remains, then, is to ask whether the Christian's distinctive calling allows him to participate in legitimate governmental uses of limited force. That is a question to which I will respond affirmatively. Yet I want the pacifist to keep disagreeing. Our society needs, as do we all, his persistent call to peace.

A Preventive War Response

Harold O. J. Brown

Although Dr. Augsburger makes much the same recommendation as Dr. Hoyt, he makes it for a radically different reason. Both Hoyt and Augsburger are convinced that the gospel forbids violence. Hoyt sees it as forbidding violence only for Christians, and as a Christian he therefore refuses to participate in it. Augsburger sees the New Testament as applicable in principle to the whole society, and since he believes that it forbids all recourse to force and armed conflict, he wants all human society to be pacifist.

Augsburger's concept of the millennium permits him to expect great social progress before Christ's return. The practical consequence is this: while Hoyt is nonresistant himself, he vigorously opposes foreign aggression and wants his own society to be defended. Hence Hoyt is rather like the fighting chaplain who feels that his duty excludes combat, but whose hatred for evil encourages him to cheer on the fighting. He puts all Christians who share his view in a kind of special class of clergy in an unbelieving secular world.

Augsburger, by contrast, is more of a true pacifist—a designation Hoyt rejects. Augsburger in effect argues that national defense should be as weak as possible, preferably nonexistent.

I think that Hoyt's views are rather inconsistent by comparison with Augsburger's, but they are less dangerous to society. Between the point at which a nation's defense is so strong that no one dares attack it (call this point A) and the point at which it is so weak that it invites a virtually bloodless takeover (point B), lies the very dangerous middle ground where one may have to fight and, win or lose, will suffer greatly from the combat. Since—short of converting everyone to Christian pacifism—our nation is not likely ever to arrive at point B, for Augsburger's arguments to push us measurably closer to it without getting us there is to make it more likely that we will be involved in a costly and perhaps unsuccessful resistance to aggression. Therefore, as a matter of prudence—a valid consideration for the Christian statesman—Augsburger's consistent, generalized pacifism is more dangerous than Hoyt's reservation of nonresistance for the aristocracy of believers.

I agree, however, with Augsburger that Christians who know the will of God cannot advocate obedience to it for themselves alone—or, as Augsburger writes in an allusion to Hoyt's dispensationalism, reserve it for a future millennium. As Augsburger says, "Whatever the meaning of the millennium, this does not permit us to postpone, as though they are only applicable in a future millennium, the implications of the Sermon on the Mount and Jesus' ethical teachings." My disagreement with Augsburger is with his contention that in this present evil, fallen world God expects and requires pacifism. This contention is, it seems to me, utopian, not biblical.

Not Enough Evidence
Augsburger proposes to deal with what he says the New Testament actually teaches—for example, its condemnation

of violence—rather than to allow his opponent to build a case for just war on the Bible's failure to condemn some who fight. Unfortunately for Augsburger, however, the New Testament is not explicit or comprehensive enough in developing the "principle of love, a practice of respect for the ultimate worth of each individual." Essentially, the New Testament does not present a new principle, it fulfills an old promise.

The principle of love does not warrant Augsburger's conclusion that therefore participation in both slavery and war must cease immediately where Christians have anything to say. Slavery, of course, as involuntary servitude, is odious to us. But we accept a form of slavery—penal servitude— as a suitable penalty for certain crimes. Some pacifists oppose prison sentences as well as capital punishment; indeed some oppose *all* governmental activity as illicit. If we accept the existence of human government in a fallen world, we must accept some use of force. If we acknowledge the rightness of punishing evildoers by force—they will seldom voluntarily submit to it—then it seems possible to justify some acts of national defense in war. If we can justify the police, we can justify the army.

Here Augsburger does precisely what Hoyt has charged pacifists with doing—he elevates a general principle, really more philosophical than biblical, to an absolute, binding rule of conduct. The principle of human worth (dignity) forbids war and capital punishment. But is this so? In the case of capital punishment at least, the dignity of man, made in the image of God, is given by the Bible as a reason for executing murderers (Gen. 9:6). When we confront the execrable dishonoring of humanity under totalitarian tyranny, can we say that a war to end it is less warranted than capital punishment for murder?

Imprudent
If, for the sake of argument, we agree that the Christian must oppose war and accept Augsburger's contention that the

ethical teachings of the New Testament are to be followed here and now, we will necessarily seek to uphold pacifism and nonresistance as social policy and to oppose military preparedness and a strong defense. This is, of course, what the traditional peace churches and the new religious pacifism do, to the extent that they participate in government. (Augsburger's own Anabaptist brethren have only recently begun to speak out. On the whole, like Hoyt's dispensationalists, they used to shun political engagement.) It is at this point that Augsburger's presentation seems to me to become inconsistent and even somewhat illogical. In a series of arguments to show that certain government policies—spending for defense, neglecting world hunger—are wrong, Augsburger certainly gives the impression that the Christian, wherever God has placed him or her, even as a politician, should work against them.

In principle, I agree with Augsburger. If a Christian knows something to be wrong, he should work against it, wherever he may be. Thus Augsburger approvingly cites Senator Mark Hatfield, who, believing war and world hunger—and abortion, which Augsburger does not mention—to be wrong, works against them as a senator. But then, rather curiously, Augsburger claims that Christians may serve in government so long as they do not try to Christianize government. Elsewhere he adds that as Christians we are not here to provide an ethic for society or the state. Like Hoyt, he too seems to presuppose that Christians will always remain a "little flock" with no real voice in society. Perhaps he is right. Yet such pessimism seems to presuppose the failure of the Great Commission.

Suppose, for a moment, that a majority of the citizens in a society came to consist of believing Christians. Are they to ignore Christianity to support some other non-Christian, anti-Christian ethic? This is what many political leaders already do, saying, in effect, "As a Christian, I know thus-and-so to be wrong, but as your president, or senator, I must serve all the people [not God?], and hence I shall do it." Augsburger does not approve of Christians acting in this way, of course, and so he urges them to stay out of high office, to remain on a level where such conflicts will not arise. I doubt that there is such a level anywhere in government, but if there is, one Christian Augsburger praises, Senator Hatfield—not to mention former President Carter—has certainly advanced beyond it. As far as I can see, Senator Hatfield does seek to apply Christian values in public policy. What does one say to a Christian who becomes president? Or to a president who becomes a Christian? I would say what I believe Augsburger wants to but hesitates to say, in the light of his own separatist outlook: "If you are a Christian, act like it, wherever you are." In other words, fear God and keep the commandments even in secular office. And, to an officeholder, one might add, "And leave it up to the voters to move you out if they don't like it."

Finally, in a fallen world where man's heart is inclined to evil, the counsel of peace at any price is a recipe for subjugation. To say, as Augsburger does, that in light of the gas chambers we should emphasize peace, is at best unrealistic, at worst positively destructive. In the face of such atrocities, the preaching of peace seems to me to mock God and justice. I can agree with him that Christians should engage in positive actions of love; there is much that can be done short of war. But some provocations are too great to ignore. To say that the love of Christ "treats every person as a person of ultimate worth" is not altogether adequate, for some "valuable" angels and humans are damned. If we are to exhibit a measure of God's self-giving love here on earth, as Jesus clearly commands, does this mean that we are to forget that there is also the "wrath of the Lamb" (Rev. 6:16) and the "lake of fire" (Rev. 20:15)? Recognition of the ultimate meaningfulness of human life does not exclude a final judgement; recognition of the dignity of humanity may involve capital punishment and even war.

The Just War

The Just War
Arthur F. Holmes

War is evil. Its causes are evil, whether they be deliberate aggression, unbridled greed, lust for power, fear and distrust, an exaggerated national pride, a perverted sense of honor or some form of social injustice. Its consequences are evil, for it produces ghastly loss of life and limb; it orphans and widows and horribly maims the innocent both physically and emotionally; it cheapens life and morality; it destroys the means people count on to sustain their existence, and it produces economic disaster. Modern weaponry could decimate and even destroy the human race. And wars that are intended to arrest violence and injustice seem only in the long run to breed further injustice and conflict.

To call war anything less than evil would be self-deception. The Christian conscience has throughout history recognized the tragic character of war. The issue that tears the Christian conscience is not whether war is good, but whether it is in all cases entirely avoidable. This is largely a policy question: In the face of such outlandish evil, how should Christians act? Of course they should seek to remedy injustice, to prevent conflict, to avoid bloodshed, to alleviate suffering; but should they under some conditions go so far as to actively support military action and participate in the fighting? Is it ever better to fight than not to fight? Could participation in war perhaps be a lesser evil than allowing aggression and terror to go unchecked and unpunished?

Prelude to the Debate

This is a complex issue, and in approaching it we must make certain preliminary matters clear. First, *not all evil can be avoided.* Evil is not just an individual's problem, nor is it confined to deeds and thoughts: it is a pervasive condition of fallen human existence that riddles the political and social reality with which we are forced to contend. Real life situations are so twisted and perverted that often no altogether good option remains. We are trapped in moral dilemmas whose roots lie in the past as well as the present, such that whatever we do involves us in evil of some sort. To punish a convicted criminal and to protect the innocent, as society must, requires that we deprive the criminal of something good, something to which he or she would otherwise have a right that we must preserve, be it life or liberty or property. There is no easy way out, nor is there in the case of war. To let violence and aggression go unchecked does not eliminate the evil, nor does it leave me unimplicated if I could do something about it.

When faced with a moral dilemma such that any action I take (including the avoidance of action) has evil results, it is not enough to weigh consequences. Right and wrong are not just a matter of the good or evil we produce. They involve both act and intent. An act may be right, and be performed with right intent, and still have evil consequences. In the case of a judge sentencing a convicted felon, the sentence may be just and the intent of the judge entirely proper, yet the sentence carries bad consequences for both the prisoner and his family (who may well be entirely innocent). The rightness of an act is not determined by its consequences alone, nor by the twisted situation that evokes it, nor by good intentions alone. Moral matters are complex: they involve deontological as well as utilitarian considerations and they concern intentions as well as act and consequences.[1]

Second, we must be clear that an ethical position, such as the just war theory or any alternative to it, is *an ideal that is normative for all people* as to how they ought to act and what they should intend. It is not a description of how in fact people have hitherto acted or what they have intended, nor of how they are likely to behave. It is a norm by which to judge actions and intentions, a standard to be appealed to in moral persuasion and to be implemented by whatever legislative or other morally proper means are available. It is not therefore a valid criticism of the theory to point out the blatant disregard of it by medieval Crusaders or by both sides in World War 2 or in Viet Nam. People disobey the Ten Commandments, too, but that does not invalidate God's Law. We cannot judge an ethic by people's failures.

As with any ethic, the just war ideal is intended to be universally binding. The Christian does not have a double standard—one for Christians and one for others. God's moral law applies to all people everywhere, and all are held accountable (Rom. 1—3). The question, then, is not whether a Christian may fight, but whether anybody at all may fight. Of course, the Christian may still *choose* to go a second mile beyond what is obligatory, as is done by "vocational pacifists" who claim that Christians have a calling different from others in regard to political and military involvement. But that is a *vocational* claim not an ethical one, and the person called thereby to nonviolence cannot label all soldiering as *ethically* wrong.[2]

Third, the just war theory *does not try to justify war.* Rather it tries to bring war under the control of justice so that, if consistently practiced by all parties to a dispute, it would eliminate war altogether. It insists that the only just cause for going to war is defense against aggression. If all parties adhered to this rule, then nobody would ever be an aggressor and no war would ever occur. The basic intention of the just war theory, then, is to condemn war and to prevent it by moral persuasion. But since people will sometimes not be so persuaded, it proceeds to limit war—its occasion, its goals, its weaponry and methods—so as to reduce the evils that have not been altogether prevented.

Fourth, the just war theory insists that *private individuals have no right to use force.* That prerogative is rather entrusted to governments in the needful exercise of their duty to preserve peace and maintain a just order. The question to be faced, then, is strictly speaking *not* whether an individual, Christian or otherwise, may fight, rather it is whether government ever has the right to engage in armed conflict and whether one should participate as an agent of government in such conflicts. The answer will depend in part on how one views the political responsibilities of Christians. If Christians may properly participate in governmental tasks, and if limited uses of force are legitimate for governments, then prima facie it is right for the Christian to participate in such uses of force.

Justice and War
With these preliminaries completed, we can turn to a fuller statement of the just war view. This can best be given by means of the following rules which spell out the application of justice to war.

1. Just cause. All aggression is condemned; only defensive war is legitimate.

2. Just intention. The only legitimate intention is to secure a just peace for all involved. Neither revenge nor conquest nor economic gain nor ideological supremacy are justified.

3. Last resort. War may only be entered upon when all

negotiations and compromise have been tried and failed.

4. Formal declaration. Since the use of military force is the prerogative of governments, not of private individuals, a state of war must be officially declared by the highest authorities.

5. Limited objectives. If the purpose is peace, then unconditional surrender or the destruction of a nation's economic or political institutions is an unwarranted objective.

6. Proportionate means. The weaponry and the force used should be limited to what is needed to repel the aggression and deter future attacks, that is to say to secure a just peace. Total or unlimited war is ruled out.

7. Noncombatant immunity. Since war is an official act of government, only those who are officially agents of government may fight, and individuals not actively contributing to the conflict (including POW's and casualties as well as civilian nonparticipants) should be immune from attack.

As we shall see later, these rules pose problems of interpretation and application to modern warfare. Their immediate impact is to place severe limits on war that would prevent its lapsing into barbarism. Underlying them is a history of ethical, political and legal theory that has developed over the past twenty-four hundred years in the West and nearly a thousand years more than that if one takes biblical history into account. That the just war tradition reaches into both biblical and Graeco-Roman sources should not surprise us, for two reasons. First, the same is true of other aspects both of Western culture and of Christian theology—Graeco-Roman forms of thought have provided the vehicle of expression for a Judeo-Christian understanding. Second, while Scripture is the final (that is, decisive) authority in matters of faith and practice, it is neither the only nor an exhaustive source of knowledge about moral matters. Scripture (for example, Rom. 1—3) makes plain that general revelation attests to our moral responsibilities, and the apostle Paul indicates that some kinds of acts are "contrary to nature." Many Christian writers, including some of the Reformers, identify the Old Testament Decalogue with a natural law written into the created order and the nature of man.

These two roots—the biblical and the natural law—underlie the just war ethic. We shall look at them first separately and then as they combine in the thinking of some later proponents, from Augustine to the present.[3]

Biblical Teaching

The first biblical datum to consider is the sixth commandment. But by itself it does not help us sort through the complexity of the war issue. The Decalogue consists of general rules that are applied in their larger biblical context to concrete situations. The historical context was Israel's escape from Egypt and journey to Canaan, during which military action was a harsh fact of life. In the Mosaic Law as a whole, capital punishment was allowable for at least ten different crimes, and killing in self-defense was not a criminal offense. "Thou shalt not kill" cannot therefore be taken to rule out all killing, let alone war.

The key passage is rather Romans 13:1-7. Here the right to use arms is accorded to the civil authorities inasmuch as they are divinely commissioned to restrain and punish evildoers (1 Pet. 2:13-14). The passage pertains directly to matters of criminal justice and the civil order and only by extrapolation to international conflict. But it does make clear that for some purposes, the precise scope of which is not defined, government has the right to use lethal force. The context concerns the law of love with its repudiation of vengeful action, its concern for those who suffer, including one's enemies, and its pursuit of peace. Any use of force, then, must be kept within these limits: it can be neither vengeful nor vicious, it must be merciful, and it must seek a just peace for all concerned.

These limitations are reinforced when one considers the Old Testament attitude toward war. While military conflict is regarded as a tragic fact of life, one for which God strengthens his people and one which God uses in the execution of justice, it is nonetheless lamented as an evil from whose scourge humanity must be delivered. Israel was instructed to limit the destruction and violence involved in its conquest of Canaan (Deut. 2). David was not allowed to build God's temple because he was a man of war (1 Chron. 22:8-9; 28:3). The psalmist grieved over violence, looking to the God who makes war cease and destroys its weaponry (Ps. 46; 120). The prophets condemned its fratricide and its atrocities (for example Amos 1—2), mourned its destruction (Lam.), and gloried in the One who will finally bring peace and justice to earth so that none need even feel afraid (Is. 2:1-5; 9:1-7; 11:1-9).

The New Testament does not address the use of military force as directly as does the Old. It predicts war in the last days, but its moral teachings generally address individuals and churches rather than the governments and rulers that are the Old Testament's concern. Jesus told Peter to put away his sword (Jn. 18:1-11), for instance, and taught his disciples not to resist evil (Mt. 5:38-48). But this has to be understood in the context of what Romans 13 and analogous passages teach. Whatever broader application Jesus' words to Peter may have, plainly they do not deny to government all uses of the sword. The New Testament does teach individuals not to use violence, and Peter was forbidden its use in religious causes (see also Jn. 18:36). Some Christians therefore repudiate any individual right to use force, even in self-defense, confining it to governmental control of evildoers.

On this basis the biblical picture is as follows: (1) The use of force in resisting and punishing violence is entrusted to governments. (2) Believers in both Old and New Testaments are involved in governmental uses of force. (3) Such uses of force are to be drastically limited to what is necessary in securing peace and justice. (4) Vengeance is thereby ruled out, along with all aggression; love and mercy must temper justice.

This biblical picture basically supports the just war theory. But not all Christians will agree with this picture for two reasons. First, because of disagreement over the relationship between Old and New Testaments. Generally, the Christian pacifist appeals to the New, which in his view takes us beyond the precept and example of the Old to a law of love. The just war theorist, however, is apt to see the law of love in the Old as well as the New, so that the New fulfills, reinforces and interprets the Old rather than superseding it. The law of love is a reaffirmation of the underlying spirit of the Old Testament Law, at one with the spirit of justice rather than in conflict with it. Love as well as justice requires action to protect the innocent and to repel and deter aggression.

The second reason is disagreement over whether and to what extent the Christian should participate in government and its exercise of force. Christian pacifists in the Anabaptist tradition usually hold a doctrine of two kingdoms or two vocations: the earthly or political vocation and the heavenly or spiritual one. Christians have their citizenship and calling in the latter. For some this has meant no political involvement at all; for others it has meant limited involvement. In either case, refusal to serve in the military is based here. Christian just war theorists, on the other hand, usually hold that the spiritual is to pervade and transform the political and other earthly tasks. They therefore have a mandate for full participation in all morally legitimate governmental functions, including military action.

These two issues represent the watershed between two markedly different theologies, so that wherever classic Anabaptist (including Mennonite) theology prevails, pacifism usually results; and wherever Reformed or Thomistic, or frequently Lutheran, theology prevails, cautious participation in government and in limited war is allowed.[4] Disagree-

ment about war, then, is not just a disagreement about the
meaning of some biblical texts. It relates to entire theologies
and resultant views of the Christian's place in society. Political and legal thought as well as theology and ethics are
involved.

Graeco-Roman Sources

Christians are not alone in having a conscience about war.
Plato, both in his *Republic* and in the *Laws*, urges limits on
war, especially in fighting among the Greeks, and insists
that the only legitimate purpose of war is the restoration of
peace. Aristotle, likewise, arguing that the very nature of
man calls for a rule of reason rather than of passion or violence, limits war to what is necessary for peace. Cicero, the
Roman jurist, developed this position at considerable length
in connection with his ideal of a state ruled by reason's laws.
Nature has endowed man with a desire for peace and order
and with the power of reason that makes possible an ordered
society. True law is right reason in accordance with nature.
It is unchanging and universal. It summons us to duty even
to our enemies; it precludes treachery; it requires that even
war be governed by moral law.

The rules of war Cicero articulated were the first explicit
formulation of just war rules such as we enumerated above,
but with some marked differences from Christian versions.
In the first place, Cicero defines a just cause as the defense
of honor as well as of peace and justice. He thinks it legitimate to revenge a dishonor. Later Christian versions reject
this and confine just cause to the defense and restoration
of peace. In the second place, while Cicero talks of humane
treatment, Christian writers go further and require merciful
treatment of enemies. These differences arise from the fact
that while Cicero's just society is ruled by natural law and
reason, the Christian concept of justice is pervaded by a concept of a love, even for one's enemies, that goes the second
mile. This rules out vengeance and unconcern.

Christian Developments

Christians in the first four centuries were far from unanimous in their attitudes to war. Roland Bainton, the church historian, points out that until the decade A.D. 170-80 we are devoid of evidence. Thereafter objections to soldiering appear, especially in the Hellenistic East and among mystic and ascetic groups. He finds extensive Christian participation in war on the eastern frontier. The Roman church of the third century allowed epitaphs recording the military profession of deceased believers, while Christians in north Africa were divided.[5]

In north Africa, for example, Tertullian acknowledges that government's authority comes from God and that Christians benefit from the peace and security good government affords. But he objects to the pagan oaths and celebrations associated with military service and discusses the case of a Christian soldier who refused to wear the victor's laurel because of its idolatrous associations. A soldier who becomes a Christian may be baptized, but should leave the army. Yet, Tertullian does not condemn the one who remains a soldier. Throughout, the objection is to idolatrous acts and pagan symbols associated with military service for Rome, rather than to the government's use of force.

Origen responds to the criticism that Christians are bad citizens for opposing compulsory military service, by claiming that they take part in both government and war by their prayers. Justin Martyr observes that we who once gloried in war now convert our weapons to implements of peace. Their point is that Christians have other tasks, another calling and a higher loyalty than to Rome. That loyalty makes them nonetheless respect political authority in its appointed task.

Ambrose of Milan goes so far as to rebuke and excommunicate the Emperor Theodosius for atrocities his soldiers committed in the siege of Thessalonica, in retaliation for a minor insurrection. Yet he gives thanks for the Emperor's victory in war and eulogizes the soldiers' courage.

These examples are typical of the church fathers. They do not deny to government the right to use force, and for all their aversion to violence they do not assert that killing is under all circumstances morally wrong. Their overt objection to soldiering is to the imposition of pagan rites and oaths. Their attitude to war is different from popular pagan attitudes; instead of excitement and glorying in war, they lament its tragic character and yearn for peace. Yet they are grateful for military action that secures both peace and order.

Underlying this attitude is a twofold basis. On the one hand, they echo the biblical lament about war even while they recognize the biblical function of government in preserving peace. It is love, rather than rational laws alone, that will overcome violence and show compassion. On the other hand, they echo the natural law: Tertullian acknowledges that there is a common law of God prevailing all over the world and engraved in nature that should be our guide. Lac tantius speaks of a natural law of love, rooted in our common humanity created by God, that requires brotherly compassion toward all people, rather than hatred and violence. The natural law, then, is the Creator's law that both mandates government to defend peace and justice and commands all people to love one another. Were this law obeyed, wars would cease—which is what the just war theory itself affirms.

Augustine, writing in north Africa shortly after A.D. 400, continues this patristic approach. He, too, recognizes a natural law as well as a biblical mandate both to governments to defend peace and order and to individuals to love their enemies. And he roundly criticizes Cicero's ideal state for failing to render to God his right: how then could it be a just society? Men are ruled in any case by what they love, not by reason and its knowledge of natural law alone. But Augustine is also realistic about the twistedness of the human condition. It is not often the case that one side is altogether in

the right and the other side altogether in the wrong. Nor is it
the case that soldiers are always able to be ruled by reason or
by love, for passions are excited and the best of moral rules
and intentions may be violated. While he endorses just war
ideals qualified by love, then, Augustine advises the
Christian who goes to war to repent in advance, because the
ambiguities of the situation confuse moral issues and
because passions confuse the moral intention. He tells the
Roman General Boniface, who was later to defend Carthage
against the Vandals, that war is not a matter of choice but of
necessity, forced on us by the need to control violence in a
fallen world. It is waged only to restore peace, so he should
preserve the spirit of a peacemaker, limiting violence to what
is needed in resisting and deterring aggression, and extending mercy to the vanquished and the captive.

Augustine's insights guided much medieval thought.
Aquinas applied both natural law and the principle of love
to questions about the legitimacy of revolt against tyrannical
government and about war, including military tactics like
ambush. In the former case, since the use of force belongs
only to lawful government, he argues that if a tyrant altogether violates the natural law on which governmental
authority rests, it is legitimate only for those next in
authority to use force against the tyrant and only to re-
establish peace and justice for the common good.

The sixteenth-century Spanish theologian Francisco de
Vitoria develops the theory further. Examining King Philip's wars against the American Indians, he condemns their
lack of just cause. War, he insists, is not justified for religious
reasons (to convert the heathen) nor for economic causes (to
gain their gold) nor for political reasons (to extend the empire). The Indians, however pagan, immoral and uncivilized,
are human beings with rights equal to those of all other persons. The natural law protects them against violence and
injustice.

Vitoria also asks whether the soldier who doubts the

justice of a cause should fight. Ordinarily, one should trust the lawful government to do what is lawful. But if justice is seriously in doubt, and if careful inquiry does not allay those doubts, then the soldier should refuse to fight. Selective conscientious objection is the corollary of a just war ethic.

The groundwork by now was laid. It remained for the Spanish Catholic philosopher Francisco Suarez to systematize the details in relation to the underlying concepts of justice and love, and for the Dutch Protestant jurist, Hugo Grotius, to do a similar job in the context of religious wars that ravaged seventeenth-century Europe. Since no common religious ground could be found, he appealed to the natural law with which the Creator has endowed all men in the light of reason. Grotius's massive study, *The Law of War and Peace*, marks the beginning of a body of international law intended to control international conflict, to bring it under the rule of law, and ideally to eliminate war altogether.

The Protestant Reformers meantime addressed the problem in similar terms. While Luther says little about natural law, he expounded on Aristotle's concept of justice and extended it from just actions to just intentions. The use of the sword, he argues, is divinely entrusted to governments in order to repel injustice and keep the peace. It can, therefore, be a work of love for the common good. But only defensive war is just, including action to recover unjustly seized property from previous conflicts. This rules out religious wars, aggression and any attempt to revenge an insult. Only the highest governmental authority has the right to initiate military action, so that rebellion is always unjustified. It was on this basis that he opposed the famous Peasants' Revolt. Yet the ruler, if wrong, should be disobeyed: selective conscientious disobedience is not revolt.

John Calvin regarded natural law as the moral law of God and appealed to it along with the Scriptures in discussing the authority of government and its right to the selective use of force. War, he allows, is permitted for the defense of peace and justice. Justice means equity, and that requires punishing the aggressor as one does a criminal. Calvin, too, confines this function to the civil authorities, forbidding armed revolt on the grounds that private persons thereby usurp what is the sole prerogative of the highest political authority.

In this tradition, for he was educated by the Puritans, John Locke's famous *Treatise on Civil Government* bases the moral justification of defensive war on natural law, so that attacks on life or liberty may properly be repelled. Aggression is always unjust, and it gives the victor no rights at all over the conquered. Even in a just war, the just victor has power only over combatants, not over noncombatants (not even those who consented to aggression) and not over property. He may not impose a new government, for the citizens of a defeated state remain free and still have the right to form their own government. As for rebellion, a tyrant may not be forcibly deposed unless the just rule of law no longer exists; in such an extreme, authority reverts to the people, who may then form a new government which accordingly has the right to use force against the tyrant. But private individuals per se in a civil society may not fight.

Both in theory and in historical statement, then, the key thesis of the just war theory is that on the basis both of Scripture and of natural law, government (and only government) has the right to use armed force, and then only in the defense of peace and justice and with severe limitations on both the ends and the means adopted. Inasmuch as Christians participate in government and serve as government's official agents, then, they may—however regretfully and with however much moral caution—fight.

Difficulties

While the just war theory has played a major role in the thought and practice of the Roman Catholic Church and of

Reformed, Lutheran and other Protestant groups, it faces serious problems.

First, the natural law ethic may tend to be overly optimistic both about man's capacity to know what is right and to do what he knows. Theorists like Aquinas and Locke held that we can logically deduce an ethic from what we know of the nature of man so as to reach universal agreement about what justice is and what must characterize a just war. They thought the needed premises about man were both rationally accessible and certain, so that it remained only to draw our inferences regarding natural rights. This rationalistic optimism about the metaphysical basis of ethics has been shaken in the subsequent history of thought, and metaphysics now appears to be a much more modest undertaking: an exploration of possible modes of thought and world-perspectives rather than a demonstrative science. As a result, concepts of justice and their application to war tend to vary far more than past thinkers imagined possible. While the just war theory, therefore, is still alive and influential and while it can be supported by good reasons, its conclusions are not as readily accepted as they once were.

With regard to man's capacity to do what he knows to be right, natural-law ethics has been overly optimistic about the rule of reason over passion and about a rule of law in human society. It assumes that man is most fundamentally a rational being, ruled by what he knows—an assumption roundly rejected by nineteenth-century romanticism, by twentieth-century existentialism and by Marxism. The Christian in measure agrees about man's capacity for rational self-deception and points to the overwhelming power of evil, even of the demonic, in human experience and history. As Augustine argued against Cicero, a man is not ruled by what he knows but by what he loves.

Any Christian version of a just war ethic must take these problems into account. The idea of natural law is attractive to one who believes in an objective basis for morality, in an ordered creation that bears witness to God's will for man, and in the general revelation of moral law. But a creationally based ethic is not decisive on many matters: it can provide a mental construct, an ethical proposal, but not logically necessary conclusions. The just war theory must, therefore, be regarded as such a proposal rather than as a necessary logical deduction, and it should accordingly be evaluated in terms of how well it comports with biblical materials, as well as with the underlying concepts of justice, love and human rights. The same, of course, is true of alternative Christian approaches to war. The biblical materials by themselves are inconclusive. We therefore develop theological constructs. We draw assistance from philosophical constructs. And our judgment about the alternative views that result depends on our judgment about the theological constructs and other concepts that shape those views.[6]

While it is true that the rule of law will neither cure nor wholly control a sin-ridden society, the fact remains that in God's creation all individual and societal activities are and should be rule-governed. The role of civil law is to govern activities within a society. The role of international law is to govern the activities of an international society. The just war theory provides a basis for laws of war—not because war is good but because it must be restricted and brought more and more under control, even while we work for its total abolition. In fact, just war ideals shaped the Geneva Convention and other international agreements, as well as helping to shape army regulations in the United States and elsewhere. Law is not enough, but it does have an educative function and, with the sanctions of international opinion and pressure, it gains a deterrent function as well. At the Nuremberg trials it also exercised a punitive function in regard to war crimes.

Nineteenth and early twentieth-century liberal theology was far more optimistic than the just war and natural law theories about society's evolving under the rule of law and the rule of love into a wholly just and peaceful condition. By legislative means, reasonable people of good will might succeed in banishing war and all other social evils from the earth. The "social gospel" of that period had not sufficiently reckoned with the sinfulness of man. In reaction to its optimism, a new "Christian realism" emerged in the 1940s among neo-orthodox and somewhat existential theologians like Emil Brunner, John D. Bennett, William Temple and Reinhold Niebuhr. In a penetrating essay entitled "Why the Christian Church Is Not Pacifist," Niebuhr points out that man's sinfulness perennially erupts in violation of peace and justice, so that force must be used to control the inhumanity of man to man. Not only love and just laws are needed in a sinful world, but also the exercise of power. This, it seems to me, was recognized by men like Augustine, and incorporated into their thinking about justice and war.

Because this is a sinful world, Christian realists have contended that just war ideals are too unrealistic. This is the problem of application in a complex and violent world. In resisting the demonic force of modern warfare, it is not always possible to limit violence or to protect noncombatants or to fight only for defense, as the just war theory prescribes. Defenders of the theory, on the other hand, find Niebuhr too much the pragmatist and prefer the moral limitations of just war rules. This requires that they be applied to modern warfare. Among Protestants, Paul Ramsey has perhaps contributed most.[7] Among Catholic writers, Father John Ford outspokenly and in the midst of World War 2 vigorously condemned the obliteration bombing practiced by both the Allies and Germany.[8] The Second Vatican Council appealed to the "binding force of universal natural law and its all-embracing principles" and called for corresponding improvements in international law. As long as the danger of war remains and there is no competent international authority, the Council admitted that governments cannot be denied "the right to legitimate defense once every means of peaceful settlement has been exhausted." But it condemned total warfare and the indiscriminate destruction of cities as "a crime against God and man"; it called for disarmament with appropriate safeguards, and it advocated the development of an international authority with power to protect the security of all, along with a regard for justice.

These qualifications are, to me, necessary consequences of a just war theory. The nation-state of the nineteenth century generated nationalisms that have little basis in the nature of man and society as ordered by God. Nationalism must give way to internationalism—a concern for the common good of all peoples.

In another area of application, selective conscientious objection must be set forth as an unavoidable corollary of the just war theory. Since it is not yet recognized in American selective service legislation, selective conscientious objectors in a morally objectionable conflict must either find an exempted occupation, face imprisonment for refusing the draft or else evade the consequences of conscientious disobedience by leaving the country.[9]

The vast destructive power of modern weaponry poses special difficulties for a just war theory. The use of nonstrategic nuclear weapons against entire cities seems entirely disproportionate as a means of defense. Many just war theorists therefore adopt a "nuclear pacifism," the view that such nuclear warfare is not morally justifiable under any conditions, no matter what the military extremity. And if the use of such weapons is disallowed, then it is courting moral disaster to stockpile them. Similar conclusions apply to all large-scale ABC (atomic, bacterial and chemical) weapons. But again the question arises in the face of human fallenness and the realities of international relations, can even this degree of disarmament be achieved?

Such a question is, it seems to me, inevitable for the just war theory. If we no longer had ABC weapons, we would begin to pose analogous objections to less destructive weapons, indeed to all warfare. For ultimately the function of this view is to bring all warfare under moral judgment and to ban war altogether. The ultimate question, however, is what do we do meanwhile? In a limited war with limited ends, forced on us by violent aggression, when the alternatives are either to let unjust violence rampage unchecked against innocent populations or else to let others without our aid attempt to check the assault, can a Christian fight?

A Nonresistant Response

Herman A. Hoyt

The article entitled "The Just War" is a very thought-provoking discussion of war and its relation to the Christian. It covers a wide span of history and a wide range of issues dealing with this theme. Holmes attempts to present the movement of thought on the issue from as far back as thirty-five hundred years. He has researched the attitudes of philosophers, biblical writers and theologians. And in addition, he has cited the practices of nations, churches and individuals in this very important area. In conclusion he has set forth the present state of this issue in the thought and practice of men.

Restating the Case
Holmes begins this discussion with a positive statement: "War is evil." While this is a self-evident declaration, he supports it by pointing out that its causes are evil; its weaponry is evil; its consequences are evil; and all it seems to

accomplish is to breed further injustice and conflict. "To call war anything less than evil would be self-deception. The Christian conscience has throughout history recognized its tragic character." Then he comes to the point of this discussion: "In the face of such outlandish evil, how should Christians act? Of course they should seek to remedy injustice, to prevent conflict, to avoid bloodshed, to alleviate suffering; but should they under some conditions go so far as to actively support military action and participate in fighting?"

Rather than enunciate a clear mandate for the Christian at this point, he launches into a long discussion of the implications involved. He begins by insisting that the problem is complex, and so complex that certain preliminary matters must first be made clear. He presents four such matters, and then concludes with a series of seven rules intended to describe the operation of just war.

These rules pose an ideal situation to which modern warfare, if any, can hardly lend itself. How is it possible to apply them in such a way that warfare does not descend into barbarism? This has been the problem of political and legal theory over the past thirty-five hundred years, and it is no nearer solution. But even so, it is argued that both natural and biblical law underlie the just war.

The Biblical Material

The sixth commandment is often cited as reason for the Christian not to engage in warfare. But the command "Thou shalt not kill" has to do with personal hatred with intent to murder. It is hardly comparable with personal responsibility in warfare which does not involve personal hatred. But even under Old Testament Law, killing in self-defense was not punishable as crime.

Not till one encounters Romans 13:1-7 is the relationship of the Christian to civil government clearly brought out into the open. Here submission is commanded because civil government is ordained of God. But Christians are not commanded to obey except in matters which are right. In matters which are wrong, they are first responsible to God (Acts 4:19-20; 5:28-29). Even though the New Testament does not confront military service as such, certain principles for the believer's conduct appear. Physical force is excluded (Mt. 5:11-12). The example of Christ is held up as the proper path to follow (1 Pet. 2:18-23). To this may be added the admonition of the Lord Jesus: "Put up again thy sword into his place: for all they that take the sword shall perish with the sword" (Mt. 26:52 KJV).

Citations from the Old and New Testaments may be used to draw some conclusions as to biblical teaching. It is true that force was entrusted to governments, not to individuals. But it is not true that believers were necessarily involved in the exercise of force, even as the agents of government, in the same way in the New Testament as in the Old. It is probably true that the use of force was drastically limited, but that is not clear. As for vengeance on the part of government, there may be some reference in the Old Testament, but the New Testament is silent. While all of these things may well be essentials to a just war theory, not all Christians will agree. There are some who insist that the issues in Israel described in the Old Testament differ profoundly from the principles of the church in the New Testament. And because this is true, some Christians will insist that there should be no involvement of the individual Christian in warfare, and where it is permitted, it must be severely limited.

Reaching back into ancient history, Holmes produces evidence that Plato, Aristotle and Cicero were among those who endorsed principles for just war. Their appeal was to natural law, rather than the higher Christian concept of love.

A long history of Christian development on this theme is then cited by Holmes. The conclusion to this discussion is that Scripture and natural law support the just war theory.

Government, and only government, has the right to use armed force, and then only in defense of peace and justice and with severe limitation on both the ends and the means adopted. Even though it is to be regretted, since Christians participate in government and serve as government officials, they may fight.

Two problems confront this conclusion. The first involves the argument based on natural law. The natural law ethic has a tendency to be overly optimistic. It can seriously be questioned whether man has the capacity to know what is right. Even when right is known, it is questionable whether man has the capacity to do what he knows. This finds support in the argument of Romans 7. The second problem is stated by the Christian realist. Are not the just war ideals too unrealistic? The world is marked by complexity, and the forces arrayed against justice and peace are too great. Even liberal theologians like Niebuhr question the wisdom and workableness of the just war system. The actual developments of the twentieth century would give refutation to this proposal.

Holmes draws his discussion to a close in a rather dismal fashion. If the just war theory is to succeed, nationalism among nations must give way to internationalism. And it will, at first to a satanically organized internationalism which will plunge the world into its deepest night of military conflagration. But, thank God, that will be succeeded by an internationalism imposed by the sovereign Lord Jesus Christ. Until then, selective conscientious objection must be guarded by the Christian, for apart from that, the Christian could face imprisonment or obligatory departure from the country. The prodigious power of modern weaponry is without solution. A complete ban on atomic, bacterial and chemical warfare leaves the nation at the mercy of unprincipled nations.

The author faces the grim reality that the just war theory has little chance for success in this present time. It may be an ideal, but it is an ideal that cannot be reached in the midst of a fallen humanity, and in the midst of an age that is growing ever worse. This solemn realization seems to Holmes sufficient reason for a Christian to fight. But to me this seems like surrendering in the face of circumstances rather than coming to grips with some clear directions from a sovereign Savior and Lord.

A Christian Pacifist Response

Myron S. Augsburger

T his very incisive chapter is a careful treatment of the
just war theory. It is important reading for every student of
this issue, as it is a defense of this position.

In his introductory remarks, Dr. Holmes is very clear that
war is evil. With this clarity he then raises the question, "Is
it ever better to fight than not to fight?" He sets forth arguments to show that not all evil can be avoided, for we live
in a world where aggression and terror are part of the human
scene. Further, he states very ably the problem of moral dilemma, and shows how we are at times trapped in them. This
is the situation in which Dietrich Bonhoeffer found himself
when he wrestled with the problem of on the one hand
letting Hitler continue with his atrocities and on the other
hand taking action to end Hitler's life. The fact that Bonhoeffer did not succeed at the latter does not alter the fact
that he was wrestling with this dilemma. Holmes takes this
dilemma seriously and uses it as a means of justifying parti-

cipation in war as, at times, the lesser of two evils. My first question is whether this is the New Testament criterion for decision making.

A second concern is Holmes's affirmation that an ethical position such as the just war theory is an ideal that is to be normative for all people. As he develops this argument he states that "the Christian does not have a double standard— one for Christians and one for others. . . . The question, then, is not whether a Christian may fight, but whether anybody at all may fight." While the sentences following respect the role of the "vocational pacifist," Holmes states that those who take such a position "cannot label all soldiering as *ethically* wrong." But I must ask: Granted that there is an ultimate right and that this is known in the will of God as expressed in the Person of Christ, are there not levels of ethical commitment?

The State and the Church

A more basic criticism of Holmes's presentation is that he does not deal adequately with the concept of the separation of church and state. Although he recognizes the theological position of the Anabaptists, who held to a clear separation of church and state, he does not pursue further their view or alternate views on the same issue. The church is made up of persons who voluntarily commit themselves to Christ, and the disciplines of the people of God. Their commitment is to the highest level of ethics as known in Jesus Christ. On the other hand, the state is committed not to Jesus Christ and the highest level of ethics, but rather to the highest level that fulfills its franchise. In our setting this is a "government of the people, by the people, and for the people," and the franchise extended to the state is conditioned by the degree of Christian ethics which is influencing society. In another type of government or in a setting where the level of ethical influence by Christians is not as high, the commitment of the state is at another level.

While there is one ethic for all people, as Holmes argues, by which we shall all be judged and to which we are held accountable, the patterns and levels of life commitment do not conform to this one ethic. As a consequence, the state operates at a different level than does the church. From this perspective it would seem that Christian influence in society would help call the state to at least the level of the just war approach. On the other hand, in the same setting the Christian's ethical perception calls him to the highest level of ethical function in the will of Christ, a New Testament ethic of nonresistant, redemptive love.

Holmes properly points out that the just war theory does not try to justify war, but rather to condemn war and prevent it by moral persuasion. He carefully outlines the principles involved in the just war theory as guidelines which will serve as preventive factors. Holmes significantly uses studies from the Old Testament as the basis of the just war theory seen in Old Testament patterns. He admits that the New Testament teaches individuals not to use violence. I would have liked to see a more extensive grappling with the issue of hermeneutics. Holmes could well have picked up at this point the doctrine of the relationship between the Testaments from the perspective of God's unfolding revelation through history and the full expression of his will in Christ. He does clearly and carefully recognize the difference between the theology of the Anabaptists, "including Mennonites," and the perspectives of Reformed and Lutheran theology. It is in these differences that the issue of hermeneutics, of the relation between the Testaments, of the two kingdoms and of separation of church and state, each find expression. The difference which I have with Holmes is basically that of a theological perspective. While his treatment is carefully done, an expression of excellent scholarship and careful theology, to deal with our differences one must recognize the theological presuppositions involved as essential elements in interpreting this issue.

Lacks Realism

The extensive treatment of classical Protestant thought is well done and helpful. This is also true of the integrity with which he faces the serious problems in the just war theory: the first being the danger of unwarranted optimism about man's ability to know what is the right action in the human situation and man's ability to fulfill it. It is significant to see that the just war theory provides limitations upon human perversity and guidelines for justice, love and human rights.

Second, the author recognizes the problem of the application of this theory in a complex and violent world where it is usually impossible to limit violence to defense. In moving from this to dealing with nuclear armament and the many uses of nuclear warfare, it appears that Holmes has a problem taking the nuclear age in stride as though it were just a normal part of the development of war machinery and could also be covered by just war guidelines. A careful review of guidelines for a just war raises serious questions as to whether nuclear warfare could in any way be justified by such catagories. It appears inconceivable that more good than evil could result from a nuclear holocaust.

In his conclusion Holmes states, "the function of this view is to bring all warfare under moral judgment and to ban war altogether." However, the realism of an understanding of the separation of church and state suggests that only among the people of God could this level of brotherhood be achieved, while among governments there will "continue to be wars and rumors of wars." It appears that Holmes's statement of the objectives of the position is overly optimistic and has a similar limitation as did nineteenth-century liberalism with its unwarranted optimism about man. However, Holmes's statement that the function of this theory is to bring all warfare under moral judgment is of special value for the multitudes of people in the Christian church who have used the just war position as a means of rationalizing their participation in war. The question I must raise is whether churches ever take this view seriously enough that they pass judgment on a given war as to whether it is a just war or not. For example, why did not the leadership of the Protestant church, especially of the evangelical church of America, take a stand on whether the American involvement in a civil war in Viet Nam was a just war or not? The problem is that the American church tends to accept the government's defense of its involvement in a given war without ever facing the question of how it can answer to the lordship of Christ and still support a decision by the government for warfare.

War is the problem of man's sinfulness writ large. Confronted with the fact that we cannot escape all evil, the basic question for us is what is the most effective way of changing human lives and altering society for the good? Here the church carries additional guilt, for if the church were as willing to share its resources and personnel for the mission of Christ as it is to share them with the state in warfare, it would doubtless have had a much greater impact for good in the world than it has. We are a part of the kingdom of Christ, a fellowship which is global. The question remains, how can a conflict between nations ever justify brethren in Christ taking each other's lives?

A Preventive War Response

Harold O. J. Brown

There are, as we have noted, two different Christian approaches to the case for nonviolence or pacifism. Hoyt contends that war may be lawful for a human government and its non-Christian citizens, but never for Christians, who have a different calling that is incompatible with combat service and violence. Augsburger, by contrast, contends that war is always wrong and hence that the Christian not only should never engage in it but should do all that he can to prevent others from so engaging. Augsburger somewhat counterbalances this advice with his contention that the Christian is not to supply an ethic for non-Christian society, but basically one has the impression that while Hoyt expects that Christians will just have to get used to living with wars among non-Christians until the return of Christ, Augsburger wants society as a whole to be nonviolent, not just its Christian component. Both Hoyt and Augsburger clearly see their attitude of nonviolence or even pacifism as a consequence of the emphasis on love that the New Testament brings over and above the Old.

Basic Agreement

It is to this basic conviction that both Holmes and I take exception. As Holmes says, "The law of love is . . . at one with the spirit of justice rather than in conflict with it. Love as well as justice requires action to protect the innocent and to repel and deter aggression." All the essayists, including the two who accept a just war theory (Holmes and myself), acknowledge that in the early centuries Christians almost never were involved in the military. Holmes sees this not as normative, but as a recognition that the Christian's primary calling is as a witness, not as a warrior. The growing willingness of Christians to fight as well as to preach coincided, all of us agree, with a growing participation on the part of Christians in government, culminating, of course, with the conversion of Emperor Constantine I. This conversion, according to Augsburger, resulted in the institution of a "fallen church."

Both Augsburger and Hoyt want to call a true church out of the world. Neither, it seems to me, takes seriously enough the situation that arises when an emperor—or a president—accepts Christ as Savior and Lord and seeks to act responsibly toward him on behalf of the society he heads. If I read Hoyt and Augsburger correctly, it seems that they would expect a Christian monarch to emulate the Holy Roman Emperor Charles V and resign. It is not altogether satisfactory to appeal to the example of non-Christian and Christian exemplars of nonviolence, such as Ghandi and Martin Luther King, Jr. When Ghandi's nonviolence succeeded, India became sovereign. Later, a free India resorted to military force to annex independent Hyderabad and Portuguese Goa, to resist China and to liberate East Pakistan (Bangladesh). Martin Luther King, Jr.'s nonviolent campaign brought about the enactment of civil rights laws that now are imposed by force.

To say that Rome stopped torturing Christians because they turned the other cheek is only part of the truth. The witness of the martyrs was very important for the spread of the faith, but it was Constantine, a "politician," who stopped the persecutions, and he did so because he believed that God had enabled him to defeat his pagan rival, Maxentius, a persecutor of Christianity, at the battle of the Milvian Bridge. Some societies are capable of engaging in rather a lot of persecution without being dissuaded by the sight of sufferers turning the other cheek. In the two situations in which nonviolent tactics have been successful, that of Ghandi and Martin Luther King, Jr., one major reason for their success surely lies in the fact that the rulers against whom they demonstrated were at least nominal Christians influenced by Christian teaching.

Holmes's Position

Holmes spends less time arguing against the position of nonresistance than in attempting to show how war can be made (somewhat) just and compatible with Christian doctrine. In order to do so, Holmes draws upon classical Graeco-Roman sources, especially Cicero, and upon the concept of natural law. The just war position thus depends not only on the concept that the Old Testament has a continuing normative validity today, but also on the conviction that there is a divinely established natural law that can be perceived even by natural man. Unfortunately, as Holmes traces the attempts of Christian writers to impress their views concerning natural law, biblical principles and the concept of a just war on Christian rulers, he reveals that they have not been very successful in restraining the aggressive violence of these rulers.

Despite these failings, Christianity to some extent has succeeded in moderating the horrors of war, particularly from the time of Hugo Grotius (1583-1645) on. Whether more could have been accomplished if more Christians had adopted the nonviolent ethic of the Anabaptists and later of dispensationalists we cannot say; we can only say that such amelioration as did take place took place through the influence of Christians prepared to take an active role in society.

The advocacy of nonresistance is based on a principle that Holmes simply rejects—that Christians have no right to participate in government. Unfortunately, what has happened in the United States is that we now have many Christians in public life who act as though they really agree with Hoyt and Augsburger and believe that they shouldn't be there. However, rather than getting out, they simply try to dissociate their public function as much as possible from their Christian values. In so doing, far from setting a Christian standard for society, they cut it off from Christian values and even from natural law values such as those presented by Cicero, since they so often coincide with biblical ones. A Christian of this variety thus may be worse in public life than the proverbial good pagan.

In the last analysis, Holmes admits that his just war theory is not an answer to the problem of violence and war—I might describe it as an attempt to muddle through in as Christian a fashion as possible. I share with him the feeling that applying the theory of nonresistance will make matters worse rather than better, as it will allow evil to flourish unchecked. If the Bible clearly commanded nonviolence, then Christians would be under obligation to practice it, no matter what consequences they might foresee. As Holmes indicates, however, the Bible does not command nonviolence, as Augsburger thinks, nor does it prohibit Christians from exercising a role in civil government, as both Hoyt and Augsburger think. In conclusion, therefore, although war is a great evil, in our fallen world it seems sometimes to be necessary to engage in it in the effort to prevent a still greater evil. War is always terrible, but at least some things can be done to make it less terrible. These things can be done, however, only by Christians willing to take responsibility as active members of a society such as ours—one in which we Christians in America, nominally at least, comprise the overwhelming majority.

IV

The Crusade or Preventive War

The Crusade or Preventive War

Harold O. J. Brown

Is it ever possible to justify waging war? Unless war can be justified under some circumstances, it is pointless to talk about the special case of crusades and preventive wars. Most Christians who defend the just war theory, including Arthur F. Holmes and Paul Ramsey,[1] do so with many reservations and much reluctance.

The most common case in which war is found to be justifiable is that of a defensive war against an unprovoked act of aggression, provided of course that the defense has some chance of succeeding and that the means chosen are proportionate to the end to be achieved. Unfortunately, many of the actual war situations that arise in history will not fit precisely into any category. Hitler's invasion of Poland was an unprovoked act of aggression which ignited World War 2. However, Hitler was joined in his aggression by the Soviet

Union, which later became the ally of Poland's defender, Great Britain, when Hitler invaded Russia. At the end of the war, Stalin insisted on keeping and even enlarging the conquests in Poland that he had originally made in his alliance with Hitler, and incidentally took effective control of most of Eastern Europe in the bargain. Thus a war that was begun as a war to defend Poland against aggression wound up in a sense as a war of aggression, at least on the part of the Soviet Union, which annexed territories not merely from its German opponent, but also from nations counted as Nazi-occupied or allied with the U.S.S.R.

If we observe how hard it is to apply the carefully worked-out categories and criteria of a just war to the situations that develop in the course of an actual war, we may be inclined to look on consistent pacifism—the willingness to suffer rather than to do harm—as the only halfway consistent solution to the problem of war. On the other hand, in view of the atrocious and enduring nature of the oppression that can be suffered when one fails to resist a tyrannical enemy, pacifism in turn may seem to be the cause of greater evils than it cures.

In any event, if we are not pacifists, but instead agree in principle that there are some circumstances in which we will go to war, we immediately run into a problem. Shall we confine our willingness to go to war to the absolutely classic case of resistance to unprovoked aggression? If so, we may find either that on the one hand we must acquiesce perpetually to evils already committed or on the other that through unwillingness to anticipate an enemy, we consign ourselves to the futile defense of an already forfeited cause. If not, how shall we define the circumstances in which it is possible, or even morally preferable, to go to war when one has not been attacked? Are there cases when the principle of legitimate defense can be extended to cover situations in which there has not yet been any act of outright aggression? Two cases of "unprovoked" war are the crusade and the preventive war.

The Nature of a Crusade

By preventive war we mean a war that is begun not in response to an act of aggression, but in *anticipation* of it. A preventive war intends to forestall an evil that has not yet occurred. The expression *crusade* is less precise, for it has been used to cover phenomena as different as the historic Crusades of the Middle Ages and the evangelistic crusades of the twentieth century. Calling an evangelistic endeavor a crusade suggests a certain *militancy*, but the term would never have been adopted if it did not have some time-honored religious associations. We would not speak of an evangelistic invasion or an evangelistic blockade. But the term should not necessarily be thought to have a purely religious meaning.

It would be useful to say that a crusade is not simply to be equated with a holy war. On the one hand, the European wars of religion, culminating in the Thirty Years' War, were not crusades, although they were religiously motivated. Neither is the conflict in Northern Ireland a crusade. On the other hand, Dwight D. Eisenhower called World War 2 in Europe a crusade, and it was not primarily religious. No one called the same war waged against Japan in Asia a crusade. The European conflict was not any more religiously motivated than the Asian: why could one be called a crusade while the other was not?

Perhaps we can define a crusade as a war that is begun not in response to a present act of aggression, but as the attempt to set right a past act. A crusade is essentially an act not of conquest but of reconquest. Thus the holy wars of the Moslems that swept over Asia Minor, Africa and part of Europe were wars of fresh conquest, and thus were different in nature from crusades. Their difference lay not merely in that their emblem was the crescent and not the cross. We do not refer to missions in non-Christian countries as crusades: the term *evangelistic crusade* is reserved for campaigns intended to win back territories and hearts that once formally acknowledged the lordship of Christ.

A crusade, then, may be defined as a war waged to remedy a past atrocity, especially one recognized as such for spiritual or religious reasons. The historic Crusades were waged to remedy the Islamic conquest of Palestine, which was held to be an atrocity because it appeared to involve a spiritual conflict and the desecration of Christian holy places as well as the oppression of Christians. Eisenhower's "crusade" in Europe differed from the more ordinary war against Japan, because in Europe there was some evidence that Christianity as such was being oppressed—Nazism was a pagan ideology, with at least a latent militancy against Christianity and an active religious-racial persecution of God's Old Testament people, the Jews. The Japanese in fact were predominantly pagans, but not apostates from Christianity, like the Nazis. Their war was merely a national power struggle, not an ideological, racial or religious holy war. The territories the Japanese were claiming had never been part of Western Christendom: hence they could not be reconquered. Thus the Nazis provoked a crusade, the Japanese an ordinary war. Curiously this definition of crusade means that the closest modern parallel to the Christian reconquest of the Holy Land in 1098 is the Jewish land-taking in Palestine, beginning in 1948 and culminating with the reconquest of Jerusalem in 1967.

The term *crusade*, which implies fighting for one's faith, has become a bad word in modern English—it even sounds a little awkward when applied to evangelistic efforts. Non-Christians repudiate the idea of a military crusade as a matter of course, and most Christians hasten to announce that under no circumstances would they endorse or defend the historic Crusades of the Middle Ages. Rather than simply reject the term outright, we may put matters into perspective a bit if we observe the way in which what the Jews did in 1948 resembles what the Christian Franks did in 1098.

The Jews conquered a land and set up a new state by force

of arms, just as the Christians had done in 1098. They certainly had an old historic and sentimental claim to the land, although they had not actually occupied it for centuries. The Christians, too, could claim historic and spiritual rights there. The new state of Israel, like the Christian kingdom of Jerusalem, is an island in a hostile Arab sea, which compels modern Israel, like Christian Palestine, to be a warrior society. For many reasons, the modern Israelis seem to be more skillful at dealing with their problems than were the medieval Crusaders—but the Crusader kingdoms endured in one form or another for two centuries, and modern Israel is less than forty years old.

Drawing Distinctions

Most readers will naturally make a moral distinction between the Crusaders and modern Israel, usually to the advantage of Israel. The Crusaders were aggressively fighting for an ideal, for religion, which is wrong almost *per definitionem* in our modern, tolerant age. But what were the first modern Jews fighting for in Palestine?

If we say that going to war for the sake of an ideal is wrong, we shall not only have to condemn the modern Israelis but also the Palestinian Arabs: both are fighting for an ideal, for land and homes are available elsewhere. We shall certainly have to condemn the various guerrilla and terrorist movements around the world, to the extent that they seek to establish ideals, such as "one man, one vote" in Zimbabwe—particularly in light of the fact that ideals such as this, as actually practiced in other African states, have had little success. Indeed, most American readers condemn terrorist movements such as that in the former Rhodesia. Yet do we not at least partially share the inclination of groups such as the United Nations and the World Council of Churches to tolerate and even support one kind of terror and atrocity—the so-called revolutionary kind—while condemning any violence used to maintain the status quo?

As we seek to establish the conditions under which it might be right to go to war, let us be careful not to work out criteria to be applied selectively, namely, only to those we wish would fight, defend themselves or conquer. Sometimes our principles seem to inhibit only ourselves, as when we repudiate a crusade fought for a religious ideal but sympathize with a revolution based on a philosophical one.

A crusade, then, is a war fought to undo something that no one had the right to do in the first place. Although the term *crusade* is usually attached to a conflict with some affinity to Christian ideals or ethics, it might also logically be applied to what we generally call a "revolution" or a "war of national liberation." Revolutions and wars of liberation, too, are fought to undo past injustice and are supposedly motivated by a concern for an ethical principle (such as freedom, equality or the right to self-government) rather than for territory, power or treasure. The historic Crusades were not justifiable in terms of the just war theory, but they were *as* justifiable as many of the other wars of earlier and later times.

If we single the Crusades out for special condemnation, it may be an expression of the unthinking self-condemnation in which Western civilization now seems to revel, but it is somewhat inconsistent as long as we do not at the same time condemn other examples of ideologically motivated conflicts. Of course very few Christians and no pacifists would justify violent revolution. However, the mentality of our age seems to be such that we judge things too much by their labels. Certainly, one can imagine that the news media around the world would be much less tolerant of a crusade, labeled as such, launched by a new Christian military order to rescue persecuted Christians in Ethiopia, for example, than of Communist Cuban "assistance" in the Angolan revolution. This is not because Communists enjoy a better press than Christians—although that may be true—but because the difference in labels confuses people about the fundamental similarity of the actions.

We can imagine that if there were a bloody persecution of Jews going on anywhere in the world, considerable efforts would be made among the world's Jews to stop it, using violent means if necessary. There is considerable tolerance, worldwide, for the idea that African blacks may use violence to put an end to the repressive system of apartheid in South Africa. But there is little or no tolerance for the idea that Christians should have resorted to violence to end the oppression of Christians—and of almost everyone else—in Uganda.

It would not be worth dwelling on this point if all war were categorically wrong. But if we accept the idea that there are some conditions that are so terrible that those who suffer from them are justified in beginning a violent rebellion, and their friends in other countries are justified in bringing force to aid them, then we are not pacifists. In that case, it is unwise to deny ourselves as Christians the same recourse to force to secure justice that we allow to others. Some Christians hold that it is always better to endure violence than to perpetrate it. But if we do not agree with that, then there is no good reason to deny ourselves as Christians the same right to intervene against gross injustice that we give to others.[2]

Let us suppose for a moment that Hitler, as he hoped, had been able to make a speedy peace with Britain and France after his conquest of Poland. Let us further suppose that, having occupied territories where millions of Jews lived, he had proceeded to implement his final solution—extermination of the Jews in territories where he exercised "lawful" sovereignty. Would the rest of the world have called for a crusade against him? Would it have waited until he committed another overt act of international aggression? If Jews were as numerous in the United States as nominal Christians, would the United States have hesitated to embark on such a crusade? If Jews would so embark—and we would not fault them for it—then should we fault Christians for going to their rescue? And should we fault Christians for going to the rescue of other Christians?

We will readily concede that there is a gradation of values involved here and that there are circumstances under which no crusade would be justified. Had Hitler confined his measures against Jews to the obligatory wearing of a gold star, for example, we can hardly imagine anyone offering to wage a crusade against him. In historical perspective, we understand that the Arabs' harassment of the Christians in medieval Palestine was relatively trivial and certainly did not justify the First Crusade.

The theory of national sovereignty is usually interpreted to mean that a sovereign state can act more or less as it pleases within its own borders, doing more or less anything it likes to its own citizens as well as to whomever else happens to be there. And the theory of national sovereignty can be used to veil terrible crimes and atrocities. The Pol Pot government of Cambodia engaged in a hideous program of genocide and systematic cruelty after winning power in 1975. Although there was some outcry in the West, in general the *Wall Street Journal* was correct in writing, "In the slow pace of world reaction to events in Cambodia there is a morbid parallel to the international blindness that first met the news of the camps in Nazi Germany in which Hitler's final solution was being pursued."[3] In a remarkable turnabout, Senator George S. McGovern, who once offered to crawl to Hanoi in an effort to end American involvement in the Viet Nam War, felt that conditions in Cambodia were so terrible that they should be changed by armed force.

If your next-door neighbor began to mutilate and kill his children, you would expect the police to intervene even if you were too timid to do so yourself. Why shouldn't you be willing to take such a stand on an international scale?

If a just war can exist only when a nation seeks to defend itself against an outright act of aggression, then clearly none of the situations mentioned above could justify going to war. Yet we can imagine that an act of outright foreign aggression, the traditionally acceptable *causus belli* for a just war, could be far less dreadful in its consequences than actions taken entirely within the borders of a sovereign state. In World War 2, the Japanese briefly occupied Cambodia. Neither in Cambodia nor anywhere else in Japanese-occupied territory were atrocities planned that even begin to resemble what a Cambodian regime has done to its own people. Even where the Japanese perpetrated atrocities, it was generally in the context of active fighting or immediately after the occupation of non-Japanese territory. Can it have been right for us to engage the Japanese in World War 2 to prevent them from ruling Cambodia and yet wrong for us to do anything to stop the carnage in Cambodia which was far greater than anything the Japanese ever tried?[4] It seems necessary to say that if war is ever justified to prevent greater evil, then we can conceive of situations in which a crusade not provoked by any direct act of international aggression, might also be justified.

The Preventive War

Prior to World War 2, Japan certainly was not looking for a conflict with the United States. Because of continuing American interference, however, the Japanese government decided to go to war when it wanted to, rather than waiting for us. This is an example of what Francis Bacon had in mind when he sought to justify the concept of a preventive war against the doctrine of the medieval scholastics, who held that war could be justified only in response to an act of aggression: "There is no question, but a just fear of an imminent danger, though no blow be given, is a lawful cause of war."[5]

If self-defense is legitimate at all, then it must be legitimate to anticipate a deadly or crippling first blow. No one would expect to wait until a gun-brandishing pursuer had fired the first shot and perhaps scored a hit before shooting at him. Severely menacing behavior, depending on its circumstances and extent, is generally accepted as a legitimate basis for initiating an act of self-defense. The difficulty, of course, lies in judging the extent and imminency of the danger. As Michael Walzer writes, "Preventive war presupposes some standard against which danger is to be measured."[6] There is always a danger of reacting too soon, as well as of waiting too long. The United States would probably never have gone to war with Japan in the 1940s if the Japanese had not attacked, or so it seems in retrospect. Of course that could not have been guaranteed; the United States declared war on Germany in 1917 when there was no substantial *causus belli* other than that caused by our material support of the Allies. The attitude and record of the United States were not reassuring to Japan.

The most striking preventive war of recent times is the Six Days' War of 1967. Faced with mounting menaces from the surrounding Arab states, culminating in an Iraqi decision to place its army under Egyptian command, Israel suddenly struck out at Egypt. The fact that the combined Arab forces were so much greater than those of Israel made any hesitation that might allow Egypt to attack at their convenience seem terribly dangerous. In 1973, Israel suffered somewhat from the onus of having struck first in 1967 and no doubt felt somewhat more secure in consequence of her 1967 victory and the territorial gains it brought. As a result, Israel allowed herself to be surprised in the Yom Kippur War and paid a high price for it, although there too Israel was successful. Did Israel measure the danger accurately in 1967 and 1973? There may have been some miscalculation, but it is hard to argue that Israel did not have reason for a "just fear of imminent danger."

Two important lessons can be learned from the Six Days' War. First, for the sake of peace, it is important not to threaten someone who is very vulnerable, as that is likely to provoke a preventive attack. Second, for the sake of peace, a state that is determined to defend itself should seek to maintain a defense force that is strong enough not to be stampeded into war at the first sign of a substantial foreign menace. In this respect a weak defense is probably worse than no defense, for no defense can at worst lead to a bloodless conquest while a weak defense will lead to a bloody one.

Practical Principles
If self-defense is justifiable—and we are assuming in this argument that it is—then under some circumstances a preventive or pre-emptive strike must also be justifiable. The difficulty, as Walzer points out, lies in the standard for judging the danger. There is a Latin proverb: If you desire peace, prepare for war. In principle one might urge that the best way of preventing war is to be well and fully armed—as is Switzerland. Switzerland is surrounded by more powerful neighbors. To none of these except Austria could Switzerland pose a serious threat. In addition, the Swiss have developed a very credible record of being determined to remain neutral, something no major power can claim. No doubt any one of Switzerland's three major neighbors—Germany, France, and Italy—could overwhelm the Alpine republic. But the Swiss assure all and sundry—and believably so—that the conquest would be at tremendous cost and the victory of little value.

An unarmed neutrality may provoke attack. Norway sought to remain neutral in World War 2, as in World War 1, but its weakness prompted both Britain and Germany to invade her for their own purposes. Sweden, somewhat less strategically situated and much better armed than Norway, was left alone. Finland was well armed and courageous, but that did not prevent the Soviet attack of 1939. Perhaps if the United States had been in a good state of preparedness in 1941, Japan would never have attacked. On the other hand, one reason for the Japanese attack was

Japan's awareness that America was indeed arming.

If the lessons of history mean anything, it seems that on the whole it is good to be well armed if one wishes to avoid war. And, if at all possible, one should contrive not to appear threatening to anyone—which is easier for a small country than a large one. It is also very helpful not to be strategically important to the plans of a great power. Isolation, of course, is a help. Spain managed to stay out of World War 2, as did Portugal. There was hardly any way that Hungary, however, could have avoided it. Even if Hungary had been as well armed as Switzerland and determined to stay neutral, its exposed situation between Russia and Germany would probably have inevitably involved her in their conflict.

If one truly desires to avoid *war*, rather than merely avoiding the appearance of militarism, it seems that the exercise of diplomatic and military prudence is of considerable value. However, that same diplomatic and military prudence may incite one to engage in a preventive war under certain circumstances. If one's primary motive is to avoid injustice, then perhaps one will never consider a preventive war. On the other hand, the same zeal for justice may appear to call for a *crusade* if it should happen to be in one's power to stop terrible acts of injustice.

It may be objected that we are appealing here to considerations of prudence and human wisdom, not to absolute ethical principles. Once it has been conceded that war may be justified, it is important to recognize that the categories that permit war to be just—such as unprovoked aggression—are themselves concepts developed by human reason. War—violent, generalized armed conflict—is a primary reality and cannot be submitted totally to a theory.

A responsible soldier might refuse to take part in a war he considered unjust, but it would be very hard for a responsible statesman to refuse to launch a preventive war if he were honestly convinced that it offered the only chance for the preservation of his people. The determination of "danger" and the "only chance" is, of course, a matter of prudence. By taking this line of argument, we are in effect giving practical considerations the last word in deciding on whether to go to war or not. At this point it may be useful to break down our consideration of the morality of crusades and preventive wars into two parts: individual responsibility and governmental obligations.

Individual Responsibility

Defenders of the just war theory accept the right, or even the duty, of the Christian citizen to go to the defense of the state when it has been unjustly attacked. The difficulty is that the individual seldom has the opportunity to know which is really the aggressor. In 1939, the German government claimed that Polish units crossed the German border to provoke World War 2; in 1967 Israel at first alleged that Egypt had attacked first in the Six Days' War. Both the Six Days' War and the Polish campaign were effectively over before the average soldier could clarify what was actually happening.

Walzer argues that an individual who knows a war to be unjust has the right to refuse to participate, but it is impossible to require each citizen to know the facts that will enable him to judge the justness of a particular war. In the period when he might possibly influence the decision whether to go to war, he has too little information.[7] Later, when the war has broken out, the information may not do him any good—"military necessity" will override all other considerations. An individual is morally obliged to refuse to participate in individual acts that he knows to be wrong, but he cannot be held responsible for knowing that the war itself is wrong. If he does know it and acts upon that knowledge by refusing to fight, he deserves praise. But if he obeys his orders and fights, it is very hard to condemn him. Individual responsibility means not making the decision to

launch a wrong war, when the citizen has the right to participate in decision making, and not performing wrong acts
in war. However, if a wrong decision has been made by the
government, it is hard to hold the individual responsible to
resist it.

One example from recent American history will illustrate
the predicament in which the citizen will find himself. In
1965 Congress passed the Tonkin Bay Resolution, which
gave President Lyndon B. Johnson the authority to wage
war in Indochina. Although Congress *could* have revoked
the resolution at any time, in fact no such action was taken
until *after* the United States had withdrawn on the basis
of the Paris peace accords. If even the most outspoken Con-
gressional critics of the war could not bring Congress to
revoke the war powers they themselves had granted, how
can the ordinary citizen with much less information and
with no comparable power be held accountable for assessing
the justice of the war and determining whether or not to take
part?

There are two *simple* decisions individual citizens could
make. On the one hand, they could choose consistent pacifism. On the other hand, they could determine to give un-
questioning obedience to their superiors. Both decisions
represent an abdication of moral responsibility. Of the two
decisions, pacifism is unquestionably morally superior,
in that the pacifist does not perpetrate evil, but only endures
or fails to resist it. The Nuremberg war crimes trials sought
to destroy the argument that obedience to orders relieves a
subordinate of personal responsibility. Total obedience to
superiors is not an adequate moral position, but neither is
pacifism, from my perspective. In consequence, individual
citizens are likely to be placed in situations where as a practical matter they cannot make a sound decision because
they lack either knowledge or power or both. Therefore,
it is all the more necessary for governments, or more specifically, for the individuals who act as rulers and make

collectively binding decisions, to make the greatest possible effort not to usurp or abuse the moral integrity of the citizens by compelling them to perform actions that, if fully understood, they would reject.

Governmental Obligations

Because individual soldiers and other citizens thus effectively transfer a part of their moral responsibility to their leaders, a heavy moral burden rests on those leaders, not only for what they themselves do but for what their subordinates do in obedience to them. The biblical concept that rulers should shun the wine and strong drink that are licit for ordinary people (Prov. 31:4-5) is explicitly based on the conviction that their greater responsibilities oblige them to maintain the greatest possible clarity of judgment. Biblically speaking, then, rulers should be held to the opposite of the privileges of rank—an exemplary servant mentality and conduct like that exhibited by Jesus himself (Jn. 13:2-17).

Practically, it seems highly desirable to have in leadership positions men and women who are personally committed to obedience to God and to biblical standards of justice. President Carter's promise of "a government as good as its people" should be raised to "a government better than its people." In contemporary American life, we have a horror of the Puritan, the moralist, in power. We extol the pragmatist, the practical man or woman of decision and action. But it is precisely the pragmatist who will ignore the moral dimensions of social problems—including war—and confront the individual citizen with a moral dilemma he or she can hardly resolve. And it is probably only the Christian in public office who can lay claim to the authority and strength to make, on the grounds of principle rather than pragmatism, a decision affecting the nation.

Individual Christians—as well as any other ethically responsible citizens—who are not willing to accept absolute pacifism as their standard find themselves in a situation in

which they fulfill their duty to obey God and to act ethically only if they make the effort to create and preserve governmental structures that will respect their ethical integrity.
If moral decisions are important to the individual, he or she
must seek to elect leaders for whom moral decisions are also
important. An individual concerned about the morality, for
example, of mass bombing will not want to be led by rulers
who are interested only in pragmatic considerations. The
mentality of our age unfortunately, tells us that we want
"practical" men in office—precisely the ones who can be
counted on to make the kind of decision about war and peace
that will place individuals in terrible moral dilemmas.

If war cannot be abolished in this fallen world, then there
will be times for preventive action and perhaps even times
for crusades. The individual generally will not be asked his
or her opinion. This fact of the human condition means that
individuals cannot be satisfied with merely seeking to live
by biblical principles, as individuals, but must seek to place
in positions of authority those who themselves seek to act
in accordance with the same principles. In the case at hand,
this will not guarantee protection from ever being asked to
go to war, nor from being asked to engage in a preventive
war or a crusade. But it at least means that individuals will
only have to acquiesce to decisions made on an acceptable
moral basis. They will not have to give in to decisions based
on opportunistic or pragmatic grounds.

A Nonresistant Response

Herman A. Hoyt

Harold O. J. Brown has elected to discuss crusades and preventive wars in relation to the Christian. At the very outset he admits that unless it is possible to justify war, then any discussion of crusades and preventive wars would be pointless. Inasmuch as defenders of just wars do so "with many reservations and much reluctance," Professor Brown has difficulty himself in even defining with a degree of certitude the nature of crusades and preventive wars.

I am sure it is Brown's purpose to cast some light on the issue at hand and give some moral direction to Christians as they face the problem of war. But I am a bit mystified as to the base from which he proceeds. If the Bible, the Word of God, is the source from which he derives his material, very little reference is made to it. This does not mean that what he says may not in general arise out of the Scriptures. But it does mean that it is difficult to discover the precise basis for many of his remarks. So far as I was able to discover, he cited only two passages of Scripture: one from the Old Testament (Prov. 31:4-5) and one from the New Testament (Jn. 13: 2-17); and neither bore directly on the issue.

If the subject of this discussion is the Christian and war, I am at a loss to determine whether this means the attitude of the Christian toward war or the participation of the Christian in war. Both are discussed in a rather philosophical manner, with some mention of a biblical perspective, but nothing is declared with persuasiveness for the Christian who is seeking clear guidance. For those who are merely interested in the academic side with its various aspects and dimensions, there is much to stimulate the thinking. But the decision is left to the individual Christian. There is no "thus saith the Lord."

I think that underlying this discussion by Brown is the realization that wars are a fact of life. I think he would agree that the prophecy of Daniel clearly states that wars will continue to the end (Dan. 9:26 ASV). And I am sure he would agree that the words of Christ can only mean that wars will continue right down to the end of the age (Mt. 24:6-7; Mk. 13: 7-8; Lk. 21:9-10). Whether they are precipitated by Christians or the unregenerate, wars proceed out of the lusts of the fallen human heart (Jas. 4:1). The real issue is what attitude the Christian should take toward approval or participation in wars.

This problem has confronted Christians ever since the day of Pentecost. But it did not become acute until the days of Napoleon. It was then that universal conscription was introduced. This made it necessary for every Chrisian to make some sort of moral response. Up until then armies were largely made up of mercenaries and men elected to join the army. Very few Christians participated. Even taxation for warfare was limited. It was not until the American Civil War that the mobilization of all the resources of a nation came into existence; this, in some sense, affected the entire population of warring nations.

A Difficult Concept

Brown finds it difficult to define a crusade. In his estimation it lacks the precision of the definition given to preventive wars. But he finally settles for this: "a war waged to remedy a past atrocity, especially one recognized as such for spiritual or religious reasons." To support this point he cites the Crusades of the Middle Ages. They were "waged to remedy the Islamic conquest of Palestine, which was held to be an atrocity because it appeared to involve a spiritual conflict and the desecration of Christian holy places as well as the oppression of Christians. He even dares to put the invasion of Europe under Eisenhower in this class, "because in Europe there was some evidence that Christianity as such was being oppressed—Nazism was a pagan ideology, with at least a latent militancy against Christianity and an active religious-racial persecution of God's Old Testament people, the Jews."

One wonders as to whether there has ever been any real Christian crusade mounted by a nation of this world. If the Crusades of the Middle Ages actually grew out of the church, it was because the church was possessed with the idea that it was the kingdom of God on earth and therefore possessed temporal power as well as spiritual power. Any such idea as this cannot be substantiated by Scripture. And it is also certainly true that the methods that were employed were carnal and not spiritual (2 Cor. 10:2-4). Moreover, to invest the Crusades with Christian principles is to fly directly in the face of what Christ said, when he affirmed that "my kingdom is not of this world: if my kingdom were of this world, then would my servants fight, that I should not be delivered to the Jews: but now is my kingdom not from hence" (Jn. 18:36 KJV). In any event, Eisenhower's "crusade" in Europe can hardly be classified as Christian. It was a military operation of the United States government directed against the Axis powers. Any benefit to Christians and Jews was merely incidental.

And How about Preventive Wars?

Preventive wars are defined by the author as engagements "begun not in response to an act of aggression, but in *anticipation* of it." A preventive war is therefore one whose purpose is the obstruction of another evil that has not yet occurred. Two cases in point are cited to demonstrate the nature of preventive war. The first is the Japanese attack on Pearl Harbor in 1941. The Japanese were pushing a program of expansionism in the Far East, and they found that the United States was standing in the way of this program. So, realizing that military conflict was inevitable, the Japanese decided to pick the time and place for launching a war. Perhaps this instance may squeak through as legitimate. But it is highly doubtful. Most certainly there was nothing Christian or religious about this war.

Nearer at hand is the Six Days' War in the Middle East. As far as it is possible to diagnose the situation at the time, the Israelis launched the first attack on the surrounding Arab nations. There is no question about the possibility of attack from the Arab nations. I was in the region just before that war broke out, and the Arab nations were amassing forces on the borders of Israel. They were poised for attack when the Israeli armies and air force swept down upon them. The swift defeat of the Arabs did not change anything in the relationship of the Israelis with the Arabs. Six years later another war was precipitated and the Israelis almost lost. Several more years have gone by and a peaceful settlement of grievances seems to be no nearer at hand than it was thirty years ago. However these engagements are evaluated, there was nothing good or Christian about them, and one wonders how, by the use of the word *preventive*, it is possible to justify the war of 1967 in the Christian sense of the word *just*.

For the most part this discussion has not clearly distinguished between the responsibility of nations as opposed to the responsibility of individual Christians. All ethical issues that have to do with nations must be discussed in the area of reason and philosophy. There is no dictum of the Scriptures which deals with nations. In the absolute ethical sense, wars are wrong as a method of settling disputes. But God has permitted this method to be used by the kingdoms of this world as the final authority. No kingdom of this world is Christian, and therefore none would bow to the authority of God. There is a day in the not too distant future when all this will be changed. So whatever there is of practical value for nations growing out of crusades or preventive wars, these operate on the human and natural level. Two lessons have been suggested: do not threaten the nation that appears to be vulnerable, for a preventive war could be incited; and, for the sake of peace, maintain a defense force that will discourage war on the part of a hostile nation. In either or both cases, it is the government that is addressed.

This means that rulers become especially responsible. Responsible statesmen must weigh the issues in relation to their own nation. And since the nation over which they rule is a kingdom of this world, it may be that they will be forced to take a pragmatic view of things and launch a war. Even if these rulers were disposed to be controlled by moral principles, they must take the pragmatic view for the sake of their country. The moral principle, however, may result in long-delayed action, in preventive war or, best of all, no military reprisal until the act of aggression.

There still remains the response of the individual Christian. Brown has wisely pointed out that he has two courses of action open to him. He can choose on his own to espouse or reject military action, or he may give himself up entirely to the direction of superiors. Without sufficient information, he is incapable of making either choice wisely. Rarely, if ever, is sufficient information available to the average person at the outset of hostilities. This means that the rightness or wrongness of a conflict cannot be evaluated by the individual. He or she is thus left to make a choice on what appears to be right or wrong. In such a decision, whichever way he turns, he can at least rest in the assurance that he has followed his conscience. But in such a situation there may be lingering doubts as to whether he was right.

There is a better way, and that is absolute dependence on the Word of God. Brown has already suggested that this may be absolute pacifism. But not even this takes into consideration both aspects of a Christian's responsibility. A Christian's highest allegiance is to God. Christians ought not to be engaged in anything which makes them take life. On the other hand, the Word of God makes it absolutely clear that Christians have a responsibility to the state (Rom. 13: 1-7). In a time of war, they could even enter the army and perform those functions which are good. And there are many. Even if they serve as civilians, they will be performing functions that are imposed by the government and will be in submission to the Word of God. I have expounded this view here under the title of "Nonresistance."

I want to commend Brown for this very thoughtful discussion. It will undoubtedly be of help to readers.

A Christian Pacifist Response

Myron S. Augsburger

This chapter is a difficult one, both for the writer and for me since my denomination holds a different stance, being conscientiously opposed to any participation in war. Brown's stance has to do with decisions as to what type of war is best and how a preventive war may preclude a more serious outbreak of violence.

In the introduction Brown makes some cursory comments regarding pacifism. Affirming pacifism on the one hand as "the willingness to suffer rather than to do harm," he then points out that "when one fails to resist a tyrannical enemy, pacifism in turn may seem to be the cause of greater evils than it cures." While this statement appears to be proper, I must ask whether the influence of the martyrs on society has not been greater than the good influences which may have come from the Crusades. This is to say that actions of love are redemptive in society. We must affirm, just as Jesus did by dying on the cross, that we give ourselves to the way of love knowing that we do not have to live; we can die. This is directly contrary to our sense of self-preservation, but it can be a witness even to tyrannical powers that there is a higher kingdom and a greater reality to which we are responsible.

In the section dealing with crusades I found it difficult to understand why Brown would take semantic aspects of the word *crusade* so seriously and spend considerable time on the term *evangelistic crusades.* Granting his point that *crusade* connotes a certain militancy, this may well suggest calling evangelistic crusades "preaching missions." However, I in no way see a direct relationship between an evangelistic crusade and the general meaning of *crusade* as "holy war." I see more relevance in his reference to the concept of holy war which is being discussed in liberation theology as justification for the overthrow of tyrannical governments. In this sense liberation theology tends to justify violence for the overthrow of tyranny, as a means to achieve greater good. This is a position built on the premise that there is more harm to humanity in continuing oppression than that which is suffered in violence used for the overthrow of tyranny. Especially in Latin America, but also in Africa, this issue is crucial in the thinking of the contemporary church as some seek to justify the use of violence to revolutionize the social order.

My own stance is that the way of New Testament nonresistant love, or of Christian pacifism, has tremendous relevance for change in a given society, although it is costly in terms of suffering on the part of the individuals who are involved in the actions of love. This is more difficult to espouse because the "revolutionary" of love expects to suffer, while the violent revolutionary assumes his goals can be achieved while others suffer.

I think Brown could have used Harry Truman's argument for the dropping of atomic bombs on Nagasaki and Hiroshima. Truman calculated that the loss of several hundred thousand lives in this atomic holocaust was a better act than the war's continuing with an equivalent number of lives being lost in battle. The question here is this: Even if such a trade-off could be calculated, as though life were a chess game, does this decision take seriously enough the long-range effect on the human family of the introduction of nuclear warfare? Further, one might raise the question as to whether or not there were other options at that stage of the war which would have led to an early end to the conflict.

Back to Basics

The more basic issue in my response to Brown's treatise is the fact that he does not deal adequately with the theological question of the separation of church and state. He writes as though church and state are so interrelated that whatever the state does with respect to war is also the function of the church. If one assumes that the two are coterminous, then the church is fully responsible for the actions of the state in war and is an equal participant.

But if separation of church and state is not simply an ideological statement but an actual description of the function of each, then it follows that the church would look at preventive measures from another perspective. By this I mean that the greatest thing the church can do is to bring the influence of Christian love and grace to bear upon society in such a way that even the enemies of our nation may be led to respect Christian values. While we may not be able to prevent war, the actions of the church to extend its brotherhood to Christians of other nations can lead to the emergence of dynamics in each society which may be more preventive than any other measure taken.

The state, to fulfill its mandate of "protecting the innocent and punishing evil," tries to protect its shores and its people. In so doing it is conceivable that defending its shores may lead to measures that are preventive of the outbreak of war.

I find it difficult in modern times, with nuclear armament, to think of war as being a means of preventing war. Recent history has demonstrated that wars tend to escalate, primarily because they immediately involve the "big powers." If a preventive war means assistance in problems between smaller nations, it must be recognized that this immediately involves the vested interest of the larger powers. The danger in our time is that the larger powers use the small ones as pawns for their own interests. A greater witness to the world may well lie in a nation such as America, which has a significant Christian population, being so influenced by Christianity that its decisions in international relations transcend this power struggle. It would seem that a truly preventive measure could well be putting the monies which go into power struggles toward helping the needy to improve their lot and to strengthen their esteem for the human rights and freedoms which America espouses.

In saying this one must be honest about what might be called a moral dilemma as in such cases as Hitler's treatment of the Jews or the situation in Cambodia. On the latter it seems that so much cultural distance exists between us and the countries of Asia that we are incapable of relating to them in ways which could help change the patterns of violence. Lacking such social proximity, to attempt preventive war as a means of correction is little more than a gamble that could immerse us in a major war with one of the big powers, with our action being termed a war of aggression. From this perspective it appears more important for us to put energies and expense into building a greater sense of social affinity with needy areas of the world. This calls for care that we not be interpreted as exploiting them. It means discovering ways in which we can extend our principles of concern for human rights to levels of human well-being. Thus, a foreign-aid program may be a far more legitimate use of funds than a program which seeks to achieve our goals by violence.

To Arm or Not

The argument that it is necessary to have a strong defense if we are to have a measure of peace is not an easy one to gainsay. During the Viet Nam War, I had the privilege of having a private discussion on this issue with then Secretary of Defense Melvin Laird at the Pentagon. I was concerned to share our church's desire for the cessation of the war and for peace and humane treatment of these people. Laird's argument for a strong armament and defense was primarily that only with such a defense can our president negotiate with the other great powers and thereby prevent more expressions of violence and warfare. Here I recall the words of Jesus which emphasize that violence begets violence. Once we commit ourselves to the path of increased armaments we encourage competition for armaments between nations.

But my theology does not ask the church to tell the state how to arm itself for the fulfillment of its mandate of defending its shores. Rather, a theology of separation of church and state calls us to wrestle with the question of how the church can be the church, both in relation to the state and in relation to its global mission of strengthening the churches in other countries, in being a brother to people of any and all nations of the world. This calls for creative, sacrificial action on the part of Christians through whom the church will fulfill its role directly and creatively. One of the problems in America is that the Christian church appears to have surrendered its responsibility to share the global fellowship of the kingdom of Christ, and it instead functions as though its relation to other peoples is primarily through channels of state.

In the conclusion of the paper Brown expresses respect for consistent pacifists as morally superior to those who unthinkingly participate in preventive wars or even in a so-called just war. He appears, however, to take the same position as does Reinhold Niebuhr, who says that it is good to have those with pacifist convictions to elevate the moral idealism of society in general, but that such pacifism is irrelevant and will not work in real-life situations. Once again we are left with questions on what is the way of the cross. The cross shows that we do not have to win or succeed (as the world speaks of success), but rather that we must simply be faithful. The most important witness to society and to the world is that of faithful Christians who would rather die than violate the nature of the kingdom of Christ to which they belong.

Reading Brown's paper I am convicted that the church needs to take more seriously preventive measures, or what we might call "preventive maintenance," in the social scene rather than emphasizing programs of "health care" which only help after the fact. If we take this seriously it could revolutionize the evangelistic and missionary programs of the church because it would force us to give more attention to meeting people's needs than to following dynamic religious leaders and their self-aggrandizing programs. The pattern of the Master still confronts us: Do we give ourselves to serve others, so that they come to know the Person and love of God? Or do we try to build a following for ourselves? James's question is still relevant: "From whence come wars and fighting among you? come they not hence, even of your lusts that war in your members?" (Jas. 4:1 KJV).

A Just War Response

Arthur F. Holmes

Can a just war theory handle the nasty complexities of historical situations? Harold Brown questions it. At the same time he assumes in just war fashion that war needs moral justification,[1] and that it is in fact justified for defense against unprovoked acts of aggression. Hence, rather than rejecting the just war position, he attempts to extend its permission to crusades and preventive wars. The issue here is the scope of a "just cause" for going to war.[2]

What Is a Crusade?

Brown defines a crusade in the following ways:

1. "An act not of conquest but of reconquest."
2. "A war waged to remedy a past atrocity, especially one recognized as such for spiritual or religious reasons."
3. "Fighting for one's faith . . . for an ideal."
4. "A war fought to undo something that no one had the right to do in the first place."

Of these, definition (1) is neither sufficient to delineate a crusade from other reconquests nor is it necessary to the definition if atrocities also might justify a crusade. Definition (4) likewise is insufficient, for any just war aimed at repelling aggression and securing a just peace would qualify. Definition (3) is not sufficient either, unless one's faith and one's ideals be understood religiously: a just war, too, is for the sake of an ideal. Definition (2) comes closest to adequacy: a nondefensive war (whether of reconquest or to stop atrocities) may be justified for religious reasons.

Apparently "religious" is meant to mean Christianity. It remains unclear whether we should include modern Israel, the Arabs, revolutionary wars or anti-Communist crusades, for the essay dismisses these with a rhetoric designed to allow Christian crusades on the same terms as other crusades, rather than ruling others out. Perhaps the intent is to advocate Christian support of military action in Uganda and Cambodia.

A crusade, then, may be either a reconquest or else a remedy for atrocity, but it must be engaged in for religious reasons. If reconquest is the case, then the crusade is against apostates rather than pagans. Yet, if atrocity is the cause, then the crusade may well be against pagans. Since at least the early sixteenth century (not, as Brown states, because of "a modern tolerant age"), the just war theory has repudiated religious and ideological causes for going to war. Francisco de Vitoria was explicit: All people have equal rights by virtue of their common humanity. Justice insists we treat equals equally. Religious differences and causes are therefore as irrelevant to the pursuit of justice as are differences of race or culture or economic status. Justice cannot allow for morally irrelevant considerations. If it be replied that we are not talking as was Vitoria of *conquest* in the name of religion, but of *reconquest* to rectify the injustice of a past conquest or atrocity, then the justice of this should be considered within just war rubrics. The reconquest of Europe in World War 2 by the Western Allies, for example, seems justified as a defense against past aggression and with the intent of securing a just peace for all concerned. That Russia violated this intent no more invalidates the just war idea than acts of adultery and theft invalidate the Ten Commandments.

In addition, both biblically and in just wars, the use of the sword is entrusted to governments, not to private parties or religious agencies. A crusade assumes either that private parties or agencies adopt force or else that government adopts religious causes. The first is illegal and (by just war principles) immoral, and it would tend to proliferate violence. The second is something neither a pluralistic society nor our constitutional separation of church and state could allow. Should the Christian, however, for religious reasons wage what to him would be a crusade, but what to others without those religious reasons would not be a crusade? In this case, he would encourage military action beyond just war limitations, which he as a Christian can justify but which neither the government nor non-Christian citizens could justify or morally support. In other words, a crusade as Brown defines it requires a kind of government and a kind of nation that in fact no longer exist. America is not a Christian nation.

Again, if a crusade is morally justified for Christian causes, why not for other causes too? Why not a Moslem crusade to destroy the state of Israel? Why not a Communist crusade (for Communism serves many of the sociological functions of religion) to retrieve ground lost to the cause in Latin America and to fight for the Marxist ideal of liberty? If we allow religious and ideological crusades, who is to say which religions and which ideals are allowed such ethical luxury and which are not?

Perhaps the Christian would like to confine it to Christianity and Christian ideals. But in the complexities of history which Brown has underscored, just how practical is such a dream? Part of the genius of the just war principle is its appeal to a *universal* ideal of justice, independent of ideological or religious differences.

Moreover, a crusade which claims exceptions to explicit just war rules as far as the *cause* of war is concerned, could also claim exceptions as far as *intent* or *means* are concerned. Unless more explicit moral limitations are forthcoming from Brown, the crusader might well adopt disproportionate means and intend far more (or less) than the restoration of a just peace for all concerned.

If war to arrest atrocities is to be morally justified, I suggest two alternative lines of argument for consideration. First, does it fit *within* just war's definition of defensive war, rather than as an extension? Does "defensive war" include defending victims unjustly attacked in a foreign country with whom we have no mutual defense treaties? I am inclined to a negative reply. This is not the right of any nation, for defensive war is by definition resistance to aggression by an outside power (or, in the case of civil war, to aggressive violence from within). However, since international law is violated, if an international law-keeping force existed, then such atrocities would amount to violence within the domain of that force and could morally be stopped by force if necessary. This is one direction in which I think international affairs could ethically move.

Second, "Christian realists" such as the Niebuhr brothers, faced with the seeming powerlessness of ethical appeals in a world of demonic violence, claim that uses of power beyond the limits of just war may well be needed. In my essay, I objected to the pragmatism of this approach. But it might be adopted if it could be kept under ethical control with the development of explicit moral limitations on any such exceptions.

What I have said reveals my concern that the "lesser evil" principle on which Brown rests his case (and which is one element in just war theory also) is by itself an inadequate basis for moral decision. To this I shall shortly return.

Preventive War or Early Defense?

Brown allows the possibility of preventive war for reasons of defense. As such it would not constitute an exception to just war guidelines so much as it would raise a question of definition: What is defense against aggression? Does it mean literally that the first blow must be struck by an aggressor, or does it allow that the aggressor's first blow be prevented? And where? In midair before the planes drop their bombs? On the aggressor's airfield when planes are being loaded? The question is often debated by ethicists applying just war rules to actual or possible situations. When the threat of military aggression is real and imminent and the aggressor's intended act would cripple defense, then "defense against aggression" might well be understood to include a preventive action.[3]

My concern is not so much over including this in the definition of defensive war as with the need for moral limitations on such a right—limitations as to timing, the extent of the attack and so on. I have less difficulty with the Six Days' War in this regard than with the Japanese attack in terms of just cause, just intention and just means. And my concern again is with the insufficiency of the "lesser-evil" principle.

The Lesser-Evil Principle

Undoubtedly, one good moral principle is that we should minimize evil and maximize good. But is this enough of an ethical framework? In a Christian ethic, is it the ultimate principle?

Stated without further elaboration, this principle could well be taken as utilitarian—that we should seek the maximum amount of good and the minimum of evil for the maximum number of people. But as any student of philosophy knows, utilitarianism does not guarantee the rights of minorities, does not define good and evil, and might allow the use of perverse means to good ends. Is the only ethical con-

cern *quantitative*, with less evil and more good? Or is it also
with the moral *quality* of intentions and acts? Is the ethic
only concerned with consequences? Or with obligations
as well? In terms of ethical theory, deontological as well as
teleological considerations count.[4]

Stated with more caution, the lesser-evil principle is sometimes treated as a principle of beneficence or love. But Brown
does not appeal to love as his governing moral principle,
nor does he seem to think Christian ethics a form of agapism;
rather his concern is to extend the *justice* of military action
beyond purely defensive moves. Yet he does not explore
the relation of the principle of justice to the lesser-evil principle. Perhaps he assumes the two are one.

The lesser-evil principle is concerned with consequences,
but justice is not primarily a matter of consequences. It is
rather concerned with the equal treatment of equals, hence
with the right of persons and the moral and legal obligations
and limitations this places on government. Brown has not
shown why it is government A's obligation or privilege to
arrest actions by government B, when B's actions do not
violate the rights of A's citizens. He has not addressed the
underlying ethical questions in political and legal philosophy.

In a biblically rooted ethic, I suggest, the two most basic
and inclusive principles are justice and love. Justice concerns the equitable ordering of a society; love has to do with
interpersonal concern and so goes the second mile in sacrificial service beyond what justice requires. But love cannot
warrant injustice. Justice tempered by love is the Christian
obligation in all situations. Hence, crusades and preventive
wars, if unjust, cannot be justified by love.

All Christian moral rules, such as those in the Decalogue,
are applications of justice and love combined. Any exception to the rule against killing must therefore be justified
by the same principles as establish the rule. The just war
theory, in Christian ethics, provides rules based on these

principles. These rules govern exceptions to the rule against killing. Any second-level exceptions (to the just war rules governing first-level exceptions) will need further investigation and support. But Brown's lesser-evil principle, at least as stated, does not ground such exceptions adequately.

I conclude that, in terms of ethics, Brown's case is at best incomplete.

Postscript: Just War and the Nuclear Threat
Robert G. Clouse

Since most Christians during the past centuries of church history have held the just war position, this closing discussion will be concerned with this view. The twentieth century requires a reconsideration of this outlook because the world situation has drastically altered. Changing technology and the dehumanizing of war have made the theories of Augustine difficult to accept. Modern weapons development which began with the invention of cannon in the fifteenth century has led to dreadful aerial bombardment in the twentieth.

New Technologies

The escalation of large-scale bombing of civilian populations is a clear illustration of the brutalizing effects of new technology on war. During the 1930s, when the Spanish town of Guernica was bombed and the Japanese used similar tactics on Chinese cities, the world responded with moral out-

rage. In 1939, after the Nazi bombings of civilian populations, President Franklin D. Roosevelt declared that:

> The ruthless bombings from the air of civilians in unforti-
> fied centers of population . . . has profoundly shocked the
> conscience of humanity. . . . I am therefore addressing this
> urgent appeal to every government which may be engaged
> in hostilities publically to affirm its determination that
> its armed forces shall in no event, and in no circumstances,
> undertake the bombardment from the air of civilian popu-
> lations or of unfortified cities.[1]

In 1940 Winston Churchill also denounced air bombardment
of cities as "a new and odious form of attack." The British
Foreign Office stated:

> His Majesty's Government have made it clear that it is
> no part of their policy to bomb non-military objectives,
> no matter what the policy of the German Government may
> be. In spite of the wanton and repeated attacks of the Ger-
> man Air Force on undefended towns in Poland, Norway,
> France, Holland, and Belgium, His Majesty's Government
> steadily adhere to this policy.[2]

Later in the same year in response to Luftwaffe attacks on
British cities the Royal Air Force began to raid German industrial cities. In 1942 the British started a policy of "obliteration bombing" intended to terrorize the German people and
reduce their "will to resist." By 1943 the United States Air
Force joined the English in obliteration bombing. On August
3, 1943 after Hamburg had been pounded by ten days of con-
centrated air raids, 60,000 acres of the city caught fire and
turned into what was to be called a "fire storm." This meant
that the entire city began to function as a huge furnace. Those
who had taken refuge in shelters were gradually roasted
alive as the temperature mounted, and others who tried to
escape the inferno were carried back into its center by high
winds. The effect at Hamburg was unintended, but the obliteration bombing of Dresden in 1945 was deliberately planned. The city was crowded with refugees and, despite later

claims that it was the center of poison-gas production, in reality it was of slight military importance. Waves of British bombers laid a fire storm over eleven square miles of the city. Temperatures soared to 1000 degrees centigrade and hurricane-strength winds swept people and objects into the core of the city. The number of bodies was so enormous that it took weeks to dispose of them and estimates of the dead vary between one hundred thousand and a quarter of a million.

During the summer of 1945 the United States Air Force unleashed an aerial attack on Japan which exceeded even that of the bombing of Germany. The culmination of this offensive came on August 6, 1945 when the first effective atomic bomb was dropped on the city of Hiroshima.[3] This blast destroyed over half of the city of 320,000, killed over seventy thousand and maimed many more. All utilities and transportation services were put out of commission and only three of the city's fifty-five health-care units were able to function. The heat was so intense that stone walls, steel doors and asphalt pavements glowed like molten iron. More than a mile from the center of the blast the intense heat fused kimono patterns on women's bodies and children's stockings were burned on their legs. After the initial blast, a fire storm raged over a mile-wide area. It was a huge, seething mass of red and purple which rose into the sky sucking into its base superheated air which burned everything combustible. The now familiar mushroom-shaped cloud hovered over the city as a symbol of the disastrous and spectacular attack. Three days later another atomic bomb was dropped on Nagasaki with similar horrible results. Aerial warfare had now been extended by technology to a fantastically effective end. One plane could do what it would have previously taken hundreds to accomplish.

Another development of the World War 2 era which has radically changed the world condition in which the just war theory operates is in the field of rocketry. The story of rocket research dates back to the early years of the century. Russians and Americans were involved in missile building, but it was in Germany under Wernher von Braun that the major advances were made. This led to the V-2 rockets which were used against England in 1944. From these beginnings came the missile programs of the United States and Russia. In 1957 the Russians orbited Sputnik and by 1961 they were able to put a manned rocket into orbit. In the same year President John F. Kennedy announced a program to put a man on the moon by 1970. These efforts, although launched for a variety of reasons including the desire to explore space and to gain a propaganda advantage, were basically a continuation of the arms race between the Eastern and Western military blocs. Rockets with even more powerful take-off thrusts were produced that could carry nuclear warheads anywhere on earth. Space satellites were launched which could be used to rain death on the enemy at a moment's impulse.

Not only did the delivery system for weapons improve but the arms have also been perfected. The bombs that destroyed Hiroshima and Nagasaki were mere pinpricks compared to present-day thermonuclear weapons. The original atomic bombs could level a city and leave a radioactive fallout in the immediate area for about a week. A twenty-megaton hydrogen bomb of the type now available can destroy a city the size of Washington, D.C., and cause serious damage over an area extending from Harrisburg, Pennsylvania to Norfolk, Virginia. Such an explosion would send radioactive fallout over an even larger area, depending on the winds. The contamination would seriously affect human beings and the earth for many generations. Stripped of emotional patriotic arguments, the use of thermonuclear bombs makes a mockery of the just war theory because it automatically causes the slaughter of noncombatants. These weapons invalidate war as a rational instrument of national policy.

Desensitization

For a while during the 1950s there was a steady stream of thoughtful criticism of nuclear warfare.[4] Gradually, however, people have learned to live with these twentieth-century emissaries of the grim reaper, and the idea of limited or tactical nuclear warfare has been advanced by such influential writers as Henry Kissinger. These conflicts would involve small "clean" nuclear weapons possessing a minimum of fallout and directed at strictly military targets. Much of the horror of nuclear destruction has been rationalized by what one writer calls "the semantics of mega-death."[5] He explains that the very nature of those weapons encourages the use of words that minimize the risks involved:

> Given the initial thrust, the makers of rhetoric in the nuclear age have shown no small measure of ingenuity in devising a jargon whose purpose and effect is to render the concept of nuclear war emotionally palatable. In the service of this objective, the existential realities of nuclear holocaust are concealed or distorted by surrounding them with a pink cloud of familiar and reassuring verbal tags .... A number of examples follow:
>
> *Clean Bomb.* A projectile which, destroying millions of people, will deposit little fallout. One thinks of scrubbed skin or of freshly done laundry, and the realities of mass death are successfully camouflaged....
>
> *Nukes.* Could anything be more deceptive than to christen weapons of mass destruction with such diminutive and affectionate labels as this?...
>
> *Hound-dog; Bambi.* Names of missiles. Underlying message: Don't be afraid of nuclear missiles: they're really cute, harmless little things....
>
> *Nuclear umbrella.* What could be more suggestive of the safe, ordinary world of daily living than an umbrella?...
>
> *Limited war.* This phrase conveys a false reassurance because it skims over the fact that even "limited" nuclear

war is still a war of indescribably horrendous devastation.[6]

Despite the new rhetoric and the fact that the world has managed to survive for several decades with nuclear weapons, the danger of a global conflagration remains a very real possibility. A clash between the superpowers would cause so much horror that there is no issue which could be solved in this way. If another worldwide conflict should occur, the earth would be in such horrible shape that it would have been better not to fight. It would seem that at this point the just war tradition would simply fade away. Yet the teaching continues among many Christians because it exists "in the realm of abstraction, where the ground of reality is lost below the cloud of hypotheses, and where any problem can be solved by the suitable manipulation of ideas."[7] In the minds of some individuals who might call theirs a just war position (though it differs from that of Holmes), the present military policies are absolutely necessary for self-defense. These people usually believe that our nation needs to be defended against Communism. Most of these writers have a very prejudiced outlook. They form their arguments in such a way as to make force necessary for the solution of problems. War must be fought to keep our nation's solemn word, or else it is the only way to defend the values of Western society. A heroic defeat is better than a disgraceful surrender, and the lands which have defended right are likened to martyrs whose influence continues through the centuries. The basic weakness of such arguments is that if thermonuclear war is allowed to occur there may not be any future generations to appreciate the present attempts to preserve Western "civilized" values.

The Contribution of Christians

The Christian as a citizen of the world as well as a member of the kingdom of heaven has many resources of peace to place at the disposal of the present age. As people who belong to a global community, the Christian church, we can advise others to avoid excessive nationalism and racism. Christ has died for all people, and it is dangerous to allow particular political problems to poison attitudes toward other racial and national groupings. Christians should also take the lead in the effort to combat hunger and poverty in the world. Wealth must be shared with others, and a more simple lifestyle is needed in the major industrial nations to preserve as much as possible of the world's dwindling resources. Secular people who emphasize a constantly increasing material culture need the Christian witness of a simple life.

Believers also ought to warn their fellow Americans against the waste and corruption of the military-industrial complex. Almost every aspect of society has rather severe economic restraints placed upon it, but in the name of patriotism and national security, high budgets are regularly voted to the military in an uncritical fashion. Those who follow Jesus Christ must be faithful witnesses to his saving power. As others accept him as Lord and Savior, they too will experience the peace of God. This will not only lead them to oppose certain aspects of the modern patriotic outlook, but also to adopt a kindly outlook even toward those they consider their nation's enemies.

William Jennings Bryan, an outstanding Christian statesman, put it this way:

No one disputes the validity of the Commandments against killing, stealing, bearing false witness and covetousness, when applied to individuals; but these commandments are not sufficiently applied to the large groups, called nations and because they are not applied there is no standard of morals which can be authoritatively invoked for the regulation of international affairs.

Men whose consciences would not permit them to take a neighbor's life, as an individual act, think it is entirely proper to take life by wholesale, either through those whom they command or at the command of others—and that, too, without regard to the cause of the war....

Men who would not think of stealing from a neighbor are taught to believe that it is patriotic to defend the taking of territory, if their nation gains by the act. Men who would shrink from slandering a neighbor seem to feel no compunctions of conscience when they misrepresent the purposes and plans of other nations; and covetousness, which is regarded as sinful in the individual, seems to be transformed into a virtue when it infects a nation. This attempt to limit the application of these commandments to small transactions has cost an enormous quantity of blood and has brought confusion into international councils.[8]

It is time we gave these commandments a worldwide scope. Individuals who follow the Prince of Peace must be in the forefront of those who work to apply the principles of love and justice not only to individuals but to nations as well.

NOTES

Introduction

[1] Peter C. Craigie, *The Problem of War in the Old Testament* (Grand Rapids, Mich.: Eerdmans, 1978), p. 50.

[2] Quoted in Stanley Windass, *Christianity Versus Violence: A Social and Historical Study of War and Christianity* (London: Sheed and Ward, 1964), p. 12.

[3] Quoted in Roland H. Bainton, *Christian Attitudes Toward War and Peace* (Nashville: Abingdon Press, 1960), p. 78.

[4] Ibid., p. 97.

[5] Ibid., p. 98.

[6] "History of the First Crusade," *The Portable Medieval Reader*, ed. J. B. Ross and M. M. McLaughlin (New York: Viking Press, 1963), p. 443.

[7] Bainton, p. 112.

[8] Thomas Aquinas, *Summa Theologica* II, ii. q. 40. For a helpful recent edition of Aquinas's work, see *An Aquinas Reader*, ed. M. T. Clark (Garden City, N.Y.: Doubleday, 1972).

[9] Quoted in Windass, p. 68.

[10] Bainton, p. 153.

[11] Ibid.

[12] Karl von Clausewitz, *On War*, quoted in Alfred Vagts, *A History of Militarism* (Cleveland, Ohio: Meridian Books, 1959), p. 182.

[13] Quoted in Bainton, p. 207.

[14] Windass, p. 107.

[15] Ray Hamilton Abrams, *Preachers Present Arms* (Scottdale, Pa.: Herald Press, 1969), p. 79.

Nonresistance

[1] Guy F. Hershberger, *War, Peace, and Nonresistance* (Scottdale, Pa.: Herald Press, 1944), pp. 57-59.

[2] Ibid., pp. 59-69.

[3] Ibid., pp. 69-72.

[4] These organizations are listed in the "Guide to Subversive Organizations and Publications," U.S. Government document, revised 1961.

Responses

[1] Schleitheim Confession, February 24, 1527; English translation by John C. Wenger, *Mennonite Quarterly Review*, 19, No. 4 (1945), 247-53.

[2] I find Hoyt's characterization of various kinds of pacifism, both its theory and its practice, quite inadequate. But I confine myself here to discussing his view of nonresistance.

[3] On this phrase, see my reply to Harold Brown in this volume.

[4]The reader is referred to George Ladd's *Crucial Questions Concerning the Kingdom* (Grand Rapids, Mich.: Eerdmans, 1952) for a nondispensational, premillennial view of the kingdom. For a discussion of the differing eschatologies presented by Ladd and Hoyt see *The Meaning of the Millennium: Four Views*, ed. Robert G. Clouse (Downers Grove, Ill.: InterVarsity Press, 1977).

Christian Pacifism

[1]Alan Walker, *Breakthrough: Rediscovery of the Holy Spirit* (Nashville: Abingdon, 1969), p. 76.

[2]For an examination of the concept of civil religion, see John A. Lapp, *A Dream for America* (Scottdale, Pa.: Herald Press, 1979); Don Kraybill, *The Upside Down Kingdom* (Scottdale, Pa.: Herald Press, 1978); Richard V. Pierard and Robert D. Linder, *Twilight of the Saints: Biblical Christianity and Civil Religion in America* (Downers Grove, Ill.: InterVarsity Press, 1978); Jim Wallis, *Agenda for a Biblical People* (New York: Harper and Row, 1976).

[3]Mark Hatfield in *Evangelism Now* (Minneapolis, Minn.: World Wide Pub., 1979), pp. 107-8.

[4]Samuel Shoemaker, *Extraordinary Living for Ordinary Men* (Grand Rapids, Mich.: Zondervan, 1975), p. 49.

[5]Malcolm Muggeridge, "Living Through an Apocalypse," *Let the Earth Hear His Voice*, ed. J. D. Douglas (Minneapolis, Minn.: World Wide Pub., 1975), p. 453.

[6]E. Stanley Jones, *Mastery* (Nashville: Abingdon, 1955), p. 309.

[7]Martin Luther King, Jr., *Stride Toward Freedom* (New York: Ballantine, 1958), pp. 81-83.

[8]For John H. Yoder's teaching see his books *Nevertheless* (Scottdale, Pa.: Herald Press, 1971); and *The Politics of Jesus* (Grand Rapids, Mich.: Eerdmans, 1972).

The Just War

[1]See for instance the classic primer on ethics by a noted philosopher, himself a Christian: William Frankena, *Ethics*, 2nd ed. (Englewood Cliffs, N. J.: Prentice-Hall, 1973). The example of the judge is taken from Augustine, who also develops the act-intent distinction.

[2]This point is effectively argued by Jan Narveson in "Pacifism: A Philosophical Analysis," *Ethics* 75 (1965): 259-71. See also the distinction between vocational pacifism and the pacifism of humanists, the liberal social gospel and the pragmatist, in Arthur F. Holmes, "War and Christian Ethics," *The Reformed Journal*, Jan. 1974, pp. 12-14.

[3]Unless otherwise noted, the materials cited appear in the anthology *War and Christian Ethics*, ed. Arthur F. Holmes (Grand Rapids, Mich.: Baker Book House, 1975).

[4]The social and cultural attitudes resulting from these theological differences are distinguished by H. Richard Niebuhr in his classic *Christ and Culture* (New York: Harper and Row, 1951).

[5]Bainton, pp. 68-84.

[6]This is a general characteristic of theoretical thought in the view of much contemporary thought: that theories are constructed and addressed in consideration both of a problem and of more fundamental beliefs. See Nicholas Wolterstorff, *Reason Within the Bounds of Religion* (Grand Rapids, Mich.: Eerdmans, 1976).

[7]See his *War and The Christian Conscience* (Durham, N.C.: Duke Univ. Press, 1961) and especially *The Just War* (New York: Scribner, 1968). The latter book deals with such complex issues as guerrilla and counterinsurgency warfare, retaliatory and preventive war, nuclear stockpiling and so on.

[8]"The Morality of Obliteration Bombing," *Theological Studies* (1944), p. 261; reprinted in *War and Morality*, ed. Richard A. Wasserstrom (Belmont, Calif.: Wadsworth Pub. Co., 1970).

[9]On this topic see James Finn, ed., *A Conflict of Loyalties* (New York: Pegasus, 1968) and Helmut Thielicke, *Theological Ethics*, Vol. 2 (Philadelphia: Fortress, 1969), chap. 28.

The Crusade or Preventive War

[1]See Arthur F. Holmes's "The Just War" in the present volume, and Paul Ramsey's *The Just War*. Holmes does not "justify" going to war, but seeks to make actual war just.

[2]This is not to argue that if others do wrong things, Christians may do them as well; what I am suggesting is that Christians accept as just or right some interventions, but then inconsistently reject their own.

[3]Leo Cherne, "The Terror in Cambodia," *The Wall Street Journal*, 10 May 1978.

[4]Of course the United States did not declare war on Japan for the sake of Cambodia, but because of the Japanese attack on Pearl Harbor. That attack, however, was the Japanese reaction to our interference with their plans for expansion in Asia; if we had not been concerned that the Cambodians—and others—not fall under Japanese rule, we would never have opposed them to the point that they felt called upon to attack us.

[5]From Francis Bacon, *Considerations Touching a War with Spain*, cited in Michael Walzer, *Just and Unjust Wars: A Moral Argument with Historical Illustrations* (New York: Basic Books, 1977), p. 77.

[6]Walzer, p. 76.

[7]Walzer, pp. 37-41, 287-303.

Responses

[1]In note #1 he claims that my version of the just war theory "seeks to make actual war just." That is not quite accurate. I regard an ethical theory, including the just war theory, as normative in the sense that just war provides a universal ideal by which to evaluate every war, possible or actual, and before which virtually every human conflict is condemned in whole or in part. It seeks to bring war under the rule of justice (defensive war only), but if every party obeyed the theory, all wars would cease. The theory's ultimate intent is accordingly the elimination of war altogether in a world of peace and justice. That it is overly optimistic, I note in my essay in the volume. But every ethical ideal is optimistic if measured by reality.

[2]While I approach the issue in these terms, later I will question whether his essay handles the matter this way at all: whether his is an ethic of justice, or an ethic of love, or both, or neither, remains inexplicit.

[3]See Paul Ramsey, *The Just War*.

[4]See Frankena, *Ethics*.

Postscript

[1]Quoted in Robert C. Batchelder, *The Irreversible Decision: 1939-1950* (Boston: Houghton Mifflin, 1962), p. 172.

[2]Ibid., p. 173.

[3]For the first atomic attack see Gordon Thomas and Max Morgan-Watts, *Ruin From the Air: The Atomic Mission to Hiroshima* (London: Hamish Hamilton, 1977).

[4]An example of this was Nevil Shute (Norway), *On the Beach* (New York: W. Morrow, 1957) a book about the last survivors of a devastating nuclear war. Another work which represents the same critical spirit was Eugene Burdick and Harvey Wheeler, *Fail-Safe* (New York: McGraw-Hill, 1962). Described as a "comic" horror story, the authors imagine that a breakdown in communication causes atomic bombers to head toward Russia with no chance to recall them. The destruction of Moscow causes the American government to drop atomic bombs on New York to avoid any further massacre.

[5]Robert W. Gardiner, *The Cool Arm of Destruction: Modern Weapons and Moral Insensitivity* (Philadelphia: Westminster Press, 1974), p. 67.

[6]Ibid., pp. 74-76.

[7]Windass, p. 145.

[8]William Jennings Bryan, "A Single Standard of Morality," *The Commoner*, 16 (March 1916) 9.

BIBLIOGRAPHY

Abrams, Ray H. *Preachers Present Arms: The Role of the American Churches and Clergy in World Wars I and II, with Some Observations on the War in Vietnam.* Scottdale, Pa.: Herald Press, 1969. Explains ways in which world war was turned into holy war and given the sanction of religion. Shows how the churches reacted to societal forces, particularly symbols and propaganda, how they were used as agents of propaganda, and their contribution to winning wars.

Adams, Robert P. *The Better Part of Valor: More Erasmus, Colet, and Vives, on Humanism, War and Peace, 1496-1535.* Seattle: Univ. of Washington Press, 1962. Gives an account of the dialogs, treatises and lectures in which these scholars sought to persuade contemporary rulers and the public of the folly of war among Christian states.

Aron, Raymond. *On War.* Trans. Terence Kilmartin. New York: Norton, 1968. Considers military possibilities which the world faces: peace, atomic war or smaller, nonatomic wars.

Bailey, Sydney D. *Prohibitions and Restraints in War.* London: Oxford Univ. Press, 1972. Discusses the just war in Christian ethics, the just war in international law, international humanitarian law, human rights in armed conflicts, arms control and disarmament.

Bainton, Roland H. *Christian Attitudes Toward War and Peace: A Historical Survey and Critical Re-evaluation.* Nashville: Abingdon, 1960. Separates Christian attitudes toward war into the categories of pacifism, the just war and the crusade. Treats the subject of war historically, bolstering arguments and conclusions by extensive research. This analysis provides an orderly framework, useful in further exploration.

Ballou, Adin. *Christian Non-Resistance in All Its Important Bearings.* New York: Da Capo Press, 1970. Reproduces Ballou's treatise on Christian nonresistance which was first published in 1846. Calls for the entire abolition of war, the armaments and preparations for war.

Bennett, John C. *Foreign Policy in Christian Perspective.* New York: Scribner, 1966. Expounds the Christian responsibility to work for a foreign policy that is as humane and just as possible. Rejects pacifism as an alternative to responsible governmental action.

_____ , ed. *Nuclear Weapons and the Conflict of Conscience.* New York: Scribner, 1962. Explores the nuclear problem in its strategic, scientific, moral and providential aspects.

Bennett, John C. and Seifert, Harvey. *U. S. Foreign Policy and Christian Ethics.* Philadelphia: Westminster Press, 1977. Discusses morality and national interest, attitudes toward war, America's political role in the world, and international ethics and economic privilege.

Best, Geoffrey and Wheatcroft, Andrew, eds. *War, Economy, and the Military Mind.* London: Croom Helm, 1976. Distinguishes between military institutions and the societies which surround them. Sees between the two a growing gap of misunderstanding and incomprehension.

Blainey, Geoffrey. *The Causes of War.* New York: Free Press, 1973. Surveys international wars fought since 1700, searching for patterns which could offer new solutions to the puzzle of war and peace.

Boettner, Loraine. *The Christian Attitude Toward War.* Grand Rapids, Mich.: Eerdmans, 1942. States the case for just war and against liberal pacifism. Sees war as being necessary at times to preserve political and religious freedom.

Booth, Herbert. *The Saint and the Sword.* New York: George H. Doran, 1923. Contains a series of addresses on the anti-Christian nature of war by the son of the founders of the Salvation Army. Considers biblical, historical and theological factors.

Booth, Ken and Wright, Moorhead, eds. *American Thinking about Peace and War.* Sussex, England: Harvester Press, 1978. Focuses on American thinking about peace and war. Contains essays by British and American scholars.

Bramson, Leon and Goethals, George W., eds. *War: Studies from Psychology, Sociology, Anthropology.* New York: Basic Books, 1964. Brings together classical and contemporary writings by psychologists, sociologists and anthropologists on the causes of war. Is primarily intended for students.

Brock, Peter. *Pacifism in Europe to 1914.* Princeton: Princeton Univ. Press, 1972. Studies the major Christian pacifist movements beginning with the early church and giving most attention to Mennonite and Quaker developments of the last centuries.

——————. *Pacifism in the United States from the Colonial Period to the First World War.* Princeton: Princeton Univ. Press, 1968. Provides a comprehensive history of pacifism covering the historic peace churches and the broader peace movements.

——————. *Twentieth Century Pacifism.* New York: Van Nostrand Reinhold, 1970. Surveys developments in the Anglo-American world with emphasis on nonviolence and active efforts to secure peace.

Brown, Dale W. *Brethren and Pacifism.* Elgin, Ill.: Brethren Press, 1970. Describes various pacifist stances, considers key ethical and philosophical issues and relates biblical themes to the present time. This work also applies the Anabaptist tradition to a radical witness in the contemporary world.

Cadoux, C. J. *The Early Christian Attitude Toward War.* London: Headley Brothers, 1919. Studies the Christian attitude toward war from the time of Jesus to Constantine. Outlines reasons Christians have accepted war.

——————. *The Early Church and the World.* Edinburgh: Clark, 1925. Examines the writings of the early church fathers on several subjects including war.

Calvin, John. *Institutes of the Christian Religion.* Ed. John T. McNeill. Philadelphia: Westminster Press, 1960. Reiterates the restraining criteria of a just war.

Clarke, Robin. *The Science of War and Peace.* New York: McGraw-Hill, 1972. Expresses concern about the threat of thermonuclear war and the arsenal of weapons created by modern technology.

Cohen, Marshall, Nagel, Thomas and Scanlon, Thomas, eds. *War and Moral Responsibility.* Princeton: Princeton Univ. Press, 1974. Contains, in Part I, a symposium on the conduct of war which examines the ethical and legal sources of restrictions on military methods and aims. Part II focuses on problems arising out of World War II and the Viet Nam War.

Craigie, Peter C. *The Problem of War in the Old Testament*. Grand Rapids, Mich.: Eerdmans, 1978. A capable explanation of the difficulty of dealing with Old Testament conflicts from a Christian point of view. Extremely helpful.

Deane, Herbert A. *The Political and Social Ideas of St. Augustine*. New York: Columbia Univ. Press, 1963. Provides a critical exposition of Augustine's social and political thought in light of his understanding of human nature.

Drinan, Robert F. *Vietnam and Armageddon: Peace, War and the Christian Conscience*. New York: Sheed and Ward, 1970. Considers the Catholic, Protestant and Jewish attitudes toward war, particularly the Viet Nam War. Covers the just war theory, the impact of revolutions, Communism, poverty and hunger. Father Drinan, a Roman Catholic priest who visited South Viet Nam, believes the church must condemn war as morally objectionable.

Durnbaugh, Donald F., ed. *On Earth Peace*. Elgin, Ill.: Brethren Press, 1978. Brings together the major documents, statements and studies that have given substance to the continuing dialog between the historic peace church (Friends, Brethren and Mennonites) and European churches, 1935-1975.

Falk, Richard A. *Law, Morality, and War in the Contemporary World*. New York: Praeger, 1963. Describes contributions that can be made by law and morality to an international regime of restraint designed to minimize the risks of nuclear war without increasing the vulnerability of nations to direct or indirect aggression.

Falk, Richard A., Kolko, Gabriel and Lifton, Robert J., eds. *Crimes of War: A Legal, Political-Documentary, and Psychological Inquiry into the Responsibility of Leaders, Citizens, and Soldiers for Criminal Acts in Wars*. New York: Random House, 1971. Discusses the problems of war crimes in terms of legal, political and ethical issues. Provides a devastating portrayal of victims and victimizers, atrocity in this technological age, and man's inhumanity to man.

Farrar, L. L., Jr., ed. *War: A Historical, Political, and Social Study*. Santa Barbara, Calif.: American Bibliographical Center, Clio Press, 1978. Suggests that a combination of interdisciplinary and comparative methods may provide the most fruitful means of understanding war.

Gardiner, Robert W. *The Cool Arm of Destruction*. Philadelphia: Westminster Press, 1974. Develops the thesis that the nation's stockpile of nuclear weapons is changing moral sensitivities, impairing judgment and reason, and anesthetizing people to the increasing danger of total destruction.

Gilby, Thomas. *The Political Thought of Thomas Aquinas*. Chicago: Univ. of Chicago Press, 1958. Expounds both the contemporary significance and timelessness of Thomas Aquinas's thought.

Greenspan, Morris. *The Modern Law of Land Warfare*. Berkeley: Univ. of California Press, 1959. States the law of land warfare including the Hague Regulations of 1907, the Geneva Convention on the wounded and sick, the Genocide Convention, prisoners of war, protection of civilian populations, and regulations affecting occupation of enemy territory and seizure of enemy property, armistice agreements and war crimes.

Gregg, Richard B. *The Power of Non-Violence*. Introduction by Rufus Jones. Philadelphia: Lippincott, 1934. Advances the principle of nonviolent resistance as an answer to the problems of war, disarmament and class struggle.

Grotius, Hugo. *The Law of War and Peace*. Indianapolis: Bobbs-Merrill, 1962. Argues that war is not exempt from legal restraint. Discusses whether war is ever justified, what constitutes a just cause, and the regulation of conduct in war.

Hershberger, Guy F. *War, Peace and Nonresistance*. Scottdale, Pa.: Herald Press, 1944. Distinguishes between biblical nonresistance and liberal pacifism.

Holmes, Arthur F., ed. *War and Christian Ethics*. Grand Rapids, Mich.: Baker Book House, 1975. Introduces influential patristic, medieval and modern writers. Tries to develop an understanding of the theoretical issues they faced while shaping a Christian criticism of war.

Howard, Michael E. *Restraints on War: Studies in the Limitation of Armed Conflict*. Oxford: Oxford Univ. Press, 1979. Discusses question of whether war can be controlled, restraints on war, limited war, wars of national liberation and war criminality.

——————————. *War and the Liberal Conscience*. New Brunswick, N. J.: Rutgers Univ. Press, 1978. Defines liberalism as the belief that humanity has the ability to improve and reach its full potential through reason. Traces the evolution of this idea as it has affected perceptions of war from the Renaissance to the present.

——————————. *War in European History*. London: Oxford Univ. Press, 1976. Studies the institution of warfare as it has developed within European society and traces its connection with technical, social and economic change.

Iklé, Fred C. *Every War Must End*. New York: Columbia Univ. Press, 1971. Explores the psychological, military and political problems which impede efforts to terminate wars.

Janowitz, Morris. *Military Conflict: Essays in the Institutional Analysis of War and Peace*. Beverly Hills, Calif.: Sage Publications, 1975. Studies both political sociology and the sociology of military institutions, war, revolutions and peace keeping.

——————————. *The Military in the Political Development of New Nations: An Essay in Comparative Analysis*. Chicago: Univ. of Chicago Press, 1964. Analyzes the role of the armed forces in the political development of new nations. Deals with the potentials and limitations of the military profession for political leadership.

Keen, Maurice H. *The Laws of War in the Late Middle Ages*. London: Routledge and Kegan Paul, 1965. Studies the law of arms, showing how the combined influence of just war theory, chivalry and regulation of military profiteering contributed to the development of the concept of effective international law.

Lamoreau, John and Beebe, Ralph. *Waging Peace: A Study in Biblical Pacifism*. Newberg, Oreg.: Barclay Press, 1980. This booklet published by evangelical Quakers contains an excellent treatment of the Bible's teaching on peace.

Lasserre, Jean. *War and the Gospel*. Scottdale, Pa.: Herald Press, 1962. Analyzes the New Testament, issuing a theological statement of pacifism. Gives special attention to the Christian's relationship to the state.

Leckie, Robert. *Warfare*. New York: Harper and Row, 1970. Describes the essentials of strategy and tactics, military formations and organizations, the evolution of weaponry, the causes of wars and their relationship to politics, issues of dissent and pacifism, and the influence of great military leaders.

Lefever, Ernest W. *Ethics and World Politics: Four Perspectives*. Baltimore: Johns Hopkins Univ. Press, 1972. Contains lectures by Lefever, Arthur Schlesinger, Jr., Paul Ramsey and Mark Hatfield addressing the topic of "morality and international politics."

Long, Edward L., Jr. *War and Conscience in America*. Philadelphia: Westminster Press, 1968. Distinguishes between "agonized participants in war," crusaders and proponents of the just war doctrine. Separates religious opposition to participation in war into three types: "vocational," "activistic," and "transmoral" pacifism.

Luther, Martin. *The Christian in Society*, Vols. 44-47 of *Luther's Works*. Ed. F. Sherman. Philadelphia: Fortress Press, 1971. Speaks not only of the act of killing but also of the moral status of the soldier and the authority of the ruler. War is justified only as a last resort, with just intent and limited means. Luther's comments on conscription and selective conscientious objection are of particular interest.

Lynd, Straughton. *Nonviolence in America: A Documentary History.* New York: Bobbs-Merrill, 1966. Traces the history of nonviolence in North America from the seventeenth century to the present.

Marrin, Albert, ed. *War and the Christian Conscience.* Chicago: Henry Regnery, 1971. Uses historical materials to clarify the various ways in which Christians have regarded war.

Martin, David A. *Pacifism: An Historical and Sociological Study.* London: Routledge and Kegan Paul, 1965. Brings sociological theory to bear upon historical materials in order to better understand modes of reasoning concerning the use of violence.

Martin, Laurence W. *Arms and Strategy: The World Power Structure Today.* New York: D. McKay, 1973. Outlines the major nuclear powers and their relationships; the types of non-nuclear limited wars and how these might occur; the key geographical areas where armed conflicts seem most threatening; and current issues such as disarmament, arms trade with the Third World, and economic aspects of military capabilities.

Mayer, Peter, ed. *The Pacifist Conscience.* New York: Holt, Rhinehart and Winston, 1966. Presents the peace plans and testimonies of the world's great peacemakers in a rich anthology.

McClintock, Robert. *The Meaning of Limited War.* Boston: Houghton Mifflin, 1967. Analyzes the pattern of limited war, emphasizing its diplomatic rather than military aspects.

Merton, Thomas. *Faith and Violence: Christian Teaching and Christian Practice.* Notre Dame, Indiana: University of Notre Dame Press, 1968. Espouses nonviolent resistance as an effective means of conflict resolution.

Myra, Harold. *Should a Christian Go to War?* Wheaton: Victor Books, 1971. Includes a statement of the pacifist position affirming the necessity for Christians to serve in the military. Concludes with a chastized promilitary position.

Nagle, William J., ed. *Morality and Modern Warfare: The State of the Question.* Baltimore: Helicon Press, 1960. Approaches the problem of modern warfare from moral, political and military viewpoints.

Nelson, Keith L. and Olin, Spencer C., Jr. *Why War? Ideology, Theory, and History.* Berkeley: Univ. of California Press, 1979. Discusses theories of war in the context of conservatism, liberalism and radicalism.

Niebuhr, Reinhold. *Christianity and Power Politics.* New York: Scribner's, 1953. Offers a collection of essays including, "Why the Christian Church Is Not Pacifist," which is perhaps Niebuhr's most direct attack on pacifism.

_____. *Moral Man and Immoral Society.* New York: Scribner's, 1932. Contends that social conflict and war are inevitable, given the self-interest and collective egoism of societal groups.

Nuttall, Geoffrey. *Christian Pacifism in History.* New York: World Without War Council, 1971. Looks at major Christian pacifist groups throughout the history of the church.

O'Brien, William V. *Nuclear War, Deterrence, and Morality.* Westminster, Md.: Newman Press, 1967. Contains an exposition of traditional Catholic thought, especially on the just war, and more recent thinking as reflected in the reports of the Second Vatican Council.

—————————. War and/or Survival. New York: Doubleday, 1969. Discusses war, deterrence, arms control and disarmament, revolution and morality.

Paskins, Barrie and Dockrill, Michael. The Ethics of War. Minneapolis: Univ. of Minnesota Press, 1979. Offers a restatement of some parts of the just war theory. Examines the extension of war beyond the battlefield by looking at three issues in some detail: the planting of bombs by terrorists and freedom fighters, the bombing by one state of the cities of another state, and nuclear deterrence.

Potter, Ralph B. War and Moral Discourse. Richmond, Va.: John Knox Press, 1969. Evaluates the reasoning processes by which individuals assess the rightness and wrongness of resorting to war and conducting war.

Rakove, Milton L., ed. Arms and Foreign Policy in the Nuclear Age. New York: Oxford Univ. Press, 1972. Gives a comprehensive and systematic view of the different positions that have been taken in regard to international relations throughout history and in modern times.

Ramsey, Paul. The Just War: Force and Political Responsibility. New York: Scribner's, 1968. Examines the morality of the use of power, calling for a doctrine of just war applied not only to military affairs but also to statecraft.

—————————. War and the Christian Conscience: How Shall Modern War Be Conducted Justly? Durham, N. C.: Duke Univ. Press, 1962. Considers theories of the just war, the use of unlimited means, and the nature of rational armament.

Rohr, John A. Prophets Without Honor: Public Policy and the Selective Conscientious Objector. Nashville: Abingdon Press, 1971. Considers whether or not selective conscientious objection should be the law of the land.

Roosevelt, Theodore. Fear God and Take Your Own Part. New York: George H. Doran, 1916. Attacks pacifism, restating Roosevelt's well-known position on immediate national issues including assuring peace through preparedness for war.

Russell, Frederick H. The Just War in the Middle Ages. Cambridge: Cambridge Univ. Press, 1975. Treats the chronological evolution of the just war theory. Concentrates on theories of the just war elaborated by scholars of the high Middle Ages.

Rutenber, Culbert. The Dagger and the Cross. Nyack, N. Y.: Fellowship Pub., 1958. Offers a biblical and theological statement of the pacifist position. Gives attention to justice and raises the question of whether humanity is moving toward a warless world.

Sampson, Ronald V. The Discovery of Peace. New York: Pantheon Books, 1973. Shifts from a study of Tolstoy's conflicting attitudes toward war to the nature and abuse of power in the modern world. Vehemently advocates pacifism.

Schlissel, Lillian, ed. Conscience in America: A Documentary History of Conscientious Objection in America, 1757-1967. New York: E. P. Dutton, 1968. Follows the course of conscientious objection as it has developed in the United States from colonial times to the present. Contains selected documents of individuals who undertook conscientious objection in times of crisis.

Shinn, Roger L. Wars and Rumors of Wars. Nashville: Abingdon Press, 1972. Narrates author's experiences as a combat soldier and prisoner of war. Also analyzes the ethics of war, discussing the forms and uses of power, conscientious objection, the possibility of nuclear war, the "glories of war," and the possibilities of a "moral equivalent for war."

Sibley, Mulford Q. and Jacob, Philip E. Conscription of Conscience: The American State and the Conscientious Objector, 1940-1947. Ithaca, N. Y.: Cornell Univ. Press, 1952. Tells the story and analyzes the problem of the conscientious objector in World War 2.

Singer, Joel D. and Small, Melvin. *The Wages of War, 1816-1965, A Statistical Handbook.* New York: John Wiley and Sons, 1972. Supplies war data in the hope of accelerating and strengthening the trend toward rigorous historical research into the causes, characteristics and consequences of international war.

Snider, Harold. *Does the Bible Sanction War? Why I Am Not a Pacifist.* Grand Rapids, Mich.: Zondervan, 1942. Evaluates modern pacifism as being unbiblical, unethical and a haven for various "isms." Sees the Bible as supporting war for righteousness, freedom, peace and honor.

Stein, Walter, ed. *Nuclear Weapons and Christian Conscience.* London: Merlin Press, 1961. Offers a rigorous presentation of the nuclear pacifist position in a series of essays by British Roman Catholic scholars.

Stoner, John K. and Schrag, Martin H. *The Ministry of Reconciliation.* Nappanee, Ind.: Evangel Press, 1973. States the case for biblical pacifism. Includes historical and theological material.

Tooke, Joan D. *The Just War in Aquinas and Grotius.* London: S.P.C.K., 1965. Examines views of Aquinas and Grotius with the aim of more ably dealing with the problem of war.

Tucker, Robert W. *Just War and Vatican Council II: A Critique.* New York: Council on Religion and International Affairs, 1966. Analyzes statements on war which were made by the Second Vatican Council, derived from a tradition in which just war concepts are pervasive.

——————. *The Just War: A Study in Contemporary American Doctrine.* Baltimore: Johns Hopkins Univ. Press, 1960. Examines the concept of just war, the moral and political dilemmas of employing force in the nuclear age, and the question of whether use of force can be sustained morally in view of the danger of a common catastrophe.

Waltz, Kenneth N. *Man, the State, and War: A Theoretical Analysis.* New York: Columbia Univ. Press, 1959. Investigates the contribution which classical political theory makes to understanding the causes of war and to defining the conditions under which war can be controlled or eliminated.

Walzer, Michael. *Just and Unjust Wars: A Moral Argument with Historical Illustrations.* New York: Basic Books, 1977. Presents a moral theory of war, focusing on the tensions within the theory which make it problematic and which make choice in wartime difficult and painful.

——————. *Obligations: Essays on Disobedience, War, and Citizenship.* Cambridge: Howard Univ. Press, 1970. Considers civil disobedience, dissent, conscientious objection, war, and revolution in relation to the individual's obligations.

Weinberg, Arthur and Lila, eds. *Instead of Violence.* Boston: Beacon Press, 1963. Contains short writings of many major advocates of peace and nonviolence throughout history.

Wells, Donald A. *The War Myth.* New York: Pegasus, 1967. Traces Western philosophical, theological and institutional justifications of war from ancient times to the present.

Wells, Ronald, ed. *The Wars of America: A Christian View.* Grand Rapids, Mich.: Eerdmans, 1981. An excellent treatment from a Christian perspective of the conflicts in which the United States has engaged. Each essay is written by a historian who specializes in the period he has covered.

Windass, Stanley. *Christianity Versus Violence, A Social and Historical Study of War and Christianity.* London: Sheed and Ward, 1964. A thoughtful argument for nonviolence from a Roman Catholic perspective.

Wright, C. Ernest. *The Old Testament and Theology.* New York: Harper and Row,

1969. States the case in chapter five for Christian participation in war based on the Old Testament image of God as a warrior.

Wright, Edward N. *Conscientious Objectors in the Civil War.* New York: A. S. Barnes, 1931. Investigates what types of individuals and which religious denominations opposed the war on conscientious grounds, what efforts were made on behalf of objectors and what changes took place in their political status, the attitude of civil and military authorities toward them, their numbers, and a comparison between conscientious objection in the Civil War and World War 1.

Wright, Quincy. *A Study of War.* Chicago: Univ. of Chicago Press, 1965. Examines the causes for war, the relation of war to capitalism and socialism, its function in society, its frequency and intensity in periods of history. Assesses the difficulties involved in all attempts to limit or eliminate war from the twentieth-century world.

Yoder, John H. *Nevertheless: The Varieties of Religious Pacifism.* Scottdale, Pa.: Herald Press, 1971. Presents the strengths and weaknesses of a variety of pacifist positions.

——————. *The Original Revolution: Essays on Christian Pacifism.* Scottdale, Pa.: Herald Press, 1971. Presents essays on various aspects of Christian pacifism including a biblical interpretation of the Old Testament and pacifism.

——————. *Reinhold Niebuhr and Christian Pacifism.* Scottdale, Pa.: Herald Press, 1954. Offers a critique of Niebuhr's position on war which reflects considerable sympathy for his insights while arguing that his position overlooks several important theological strands which justify Christian pacifism.

Zahn, Gordon C. *An Alternative to War.* New York: Council on Religion and International Affairs, 1963. Examines the theory of nonviolence against the background of threatened nuclear war.

——————. *War, Conscience and Dissent.* New York: Hawthorne Books, 1967. Presents a case against the just war, using the Catholic response to Hitler and the statements of recent popes.

Zampaglione, Gerardo. *The Idea of Peace in Antiquity.* Notre Dame, Ind.: Univ. of Notre Dame Press, 1973. Covers the Greek, Hellenistic, biblical and early church periods.

Contributing
Authors

Myron S. Augsburger was born in Ohio. He is a graduate
of Eastern Mennonite College (B.A.), Goshen Seminary (B.D.)
and Union Theological Seminary of Richmond, Virgina
(Th.M., Th.D) and has done postgraduate work at the University of Michigan and the University of Basel, Switzerland. He has conducted evangelistic crusades and has lec-
tured throughout the U.S. and Canada, as well as in Jamaica,
Europe, the Middle East, India, Africa, the Orient, Central
and South America. Currently he is president and professor
of theology at Eastern Mennonite College. His publications
include *Called to Maturity, Quench Not the Spirit, Walking
in the Resurrection* and *Faithful unto Death.*

Harold O. J. Brown has studied at Harvard University (B.A.,
S.T.B., Th.M. and Ph.D.) and Marburg University. He has
served as a minister, as theological secretary of the International Fellowship of Evangelical Students, and as associate

editor of *Christianity Today*. Presently he is professor of systematic theology and chairman of the division of theology at Trinity Evangelical Divinity School. His publications include *Protest of a Troubled Protestant, Christianity and the Class Struggle* and *The Reconstruction of the Republic.*

Robert G. Clouse is professor of history at Indiana State University, Terre Haute, and also is an ordained Brethren minister, having served churches in Iowa and Indiana. He graduated from Bryan College (B.A.), Grace Theological Seminary (B.D.) and the University of Iowa (M.A. and Ph.D.). As a student of the history of Christian thought, Clouse has edited *The Meaning of the Millennium: Four Views* and *The Cross and the Flag*. Other publications include *Streams of Civilization* (with Richard V. Pierard) and *The Church in the Age of Orthodoxy and the Enlightenment.*

Arthur F. Holmes was born in England and educated at Wheaton College (B.A. and M.A.) and Northwestern University (Ph.D.). He currently serves as professor of philosophy and chairman of the philosophy department at Wheaton College in Illinois. Holmes is the author of *Christianity and Philosophy, Faith Seeks Understanding, War and Christian Ethics* and *All Truth is God's Truth.*

Herman A. Hoyt is president emeritus of Grace Schools, Winona Lake, Indiana. He holds the A.B., B.D., M.Th. and Th.D. degrees and has written many books, two of which deal with the theme of the Christian and war: *All Things: Whatsoever I Have Commanded You* and *Then Would My Servants Fight*. Hoyt was associated with Dr. Alva J. McClain in the founding of Grace Theological Seminary in 1937.